Asa Hull

The Star of the East

A collection of Hymns and Tunes

Asa Hull

The Star of the East
A collection of Hymns and Tunes

ISBN/EAN: 9783337290115

Printed in Europe, USA, Canada, Australia, Japan

Cover: Foto ©Thomas Meinert / pixelio.de

More available books at **www.hansebooks.com**

THE

STAR OF THE EAST;

A COLLECTION OF

HYMNS AND TUNES,

SUITABLE FOR ALL OCCASIONS OF

SOCIAL WORSHIP,

AND

SABBATH SCHOOLS.

BY ASA HULL.

BOSTON:
PUBLISHED BY RUSSELL & PATEE.

PREFACE.

We have no apology to offer for adding another to the already very lengthy catalogue of Music Books, other than the universal demand for a work suitable for Social Worship, and at the same time available as a Sabbath School singing book. Our hopes of success in this department rest in a certain degree on the very general and increasing belief that the songs of Social Religious Meetings and Sabbath Schools, (Infant classes excepted,) should be one and the same.

Entered, according to Act of Congress, in the year 1861, by
RUSSELL & PATEE,
In the Clerk's Office of the District Court of the District of Massachusetts.

STAR OF THE EAST.

GLORY TO THE LAMB.

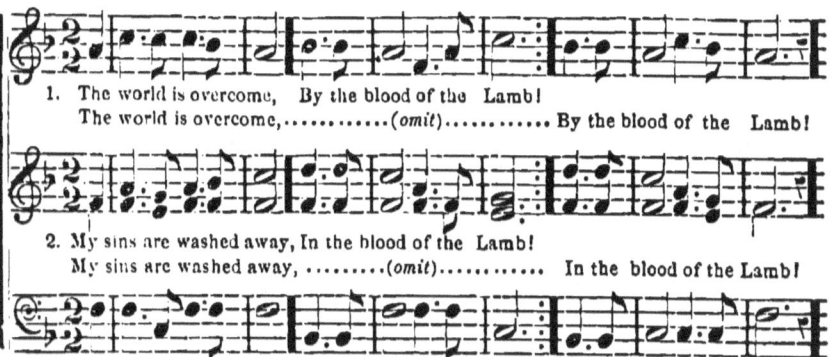

1. The world is overcome, By the blood of the Lamb!
The world is overcome,............(omit)............ By the blood of the Lamb!

2. My sins are washed away, In the blood of the Lamb!
My sins are washed away,..........(omit)............ In the blood of the Lamb!

CHORUS. With energy.

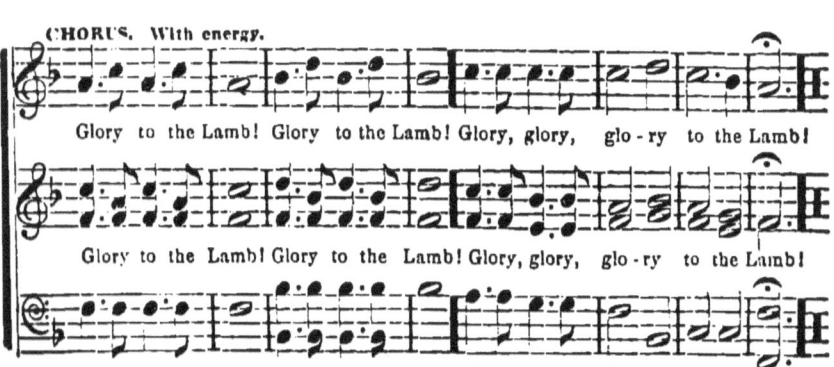

Glory to the Lamb! Glory to the Lamb! Glory, glory, glo-ry to the Lamb!

Glory to the Lamb! Glory to the Lamb! Glory, glory, glo-ry to the Lamb!

3
The devil's overcome by the blood of the Lamb! Glory, &c.

4
I've lost the fear of death through the blood of the Lamb! Glory, &c.

5
The martyrs overcame by the blood of the Lamb! Glory, &c.

6
I hope to gain the skies by the blood of the Lamb! Glory, &c.

DEAR SAVIOUR. L. M.

1. Je-sus, my all, to heav'n is gone, He, whom I fix my hopes up-on;
   His track I see, and I'll pur-sue, The nar-row way, till him I view.
2. The way the ho-ly prophets went, The road that leads from ban-ish-ment;
   The King's highway of ho-li-ness, I'll go, for all his paths are peace.
3. This is the way I long have sought, And mourn'd because I found it not;
   My grief a bur-den long has been, Because I was not saved from sin.
4. The more I strove against its power, I felt its weight and guilt the more;
   'Till late I heard my Saviour say,—Come hither, soul, I am the way.

CHORUS.

O may this heart, dear Saviour be, For-ev-er closed to all but thee;
O may this heart, dear Saviour be, For-ev-er closed to all but thee;

* Chorus set to the hymn on the opposite page can be used to all the hymns if preferred.

DEAR SAVIOUR. Concluded.

Then will I tell to sinners round, What a dear Saviour I have found.

Then will I tell to sinners round, What a dear Saviour I have found.

5.
Lo! glad I come; and thou, blest Lamb,
Shalt take me to thee, as I am;
Nothing but sin have I to give,—
Nothing but love shall I receive.
O may this heart, &c.

6.
Then will I tell to sinners round,
What a dear Saviour I have found;
I'll point to thy redeeming blood,
And say,—Behold the way to God.
O may this heart, &c.

THE YOUTHFUL PILGRIM.

1.
I would a youthful pilgrim be,
Resolved alone to follow thee,
Thou Lamb of God, who now art gone;
Up to thine everlasting throne.
O may this heart &c.

2.
I would my heart to thee resign;
O come and make it wholly thine;
Set up thy kingdom, Lord, within,
And cast out every thought of sin.
O may this heart, &c.

3.
Be it my chief desire to prove
How much I owe, how much I love;
Contentedly my cross to take,
And meekly bear it for thy sake.
O may this heart, &c.

4.
Then, when my pilgrimage is o'er,
And I can serve thee here no more,
Within thy temple, Lord of love,
I'll serve thee day and night above.
O may this heart, &c.

VOWS REMEMBERED AND RENEWED.

1.
O happy day that fix'd my choice,
On thee, my Saviour and my God!
Well may this glowing heart rejoice,
And tell its raptures all abroad.
Cho.—He taught me how to watch and pray,
And live rejoicing every day;
O happy day, O happy day,
When Jesus washed my sins away.

2.
O happy bond, that seals my vows
To him who merits all my love;
Let cheerful anthems fill his house,
While to that sacred shrine I move
He taught me, &c.

3.
'Tis done, the great transaction's done;
I am my Lord's, and he is mine;
He drew me, and I followed on,
Charm'd to confess the voice divine.
He taught me, &c.

4.
Now rest, my long-divided heart;
Fixed on this blissful centre rest;
Nor ever from thy Lord depart:
With him of every good possessed.
He taught me, &c.

5.
High heaven, that heard the solemn vow
That vow renew'd shall daily hear,
Till in life's latest hour I bow,
And bless in death a bond so dear.
He taught me, &c.

THE INVITATION.

3
Still the echoed voice is ringing,
    "Come, O come,"
Every heart pure incense bringing,
    "Hither come."

Father, round the altar bending,
May our souls to heav'n ascending,
    Find in thee their home,
    Find in thee their home.

* Treble and Tenor, will use small notes first time.

SHALL WE MEET? 8s & 7s.

Oct. 24, 1860.

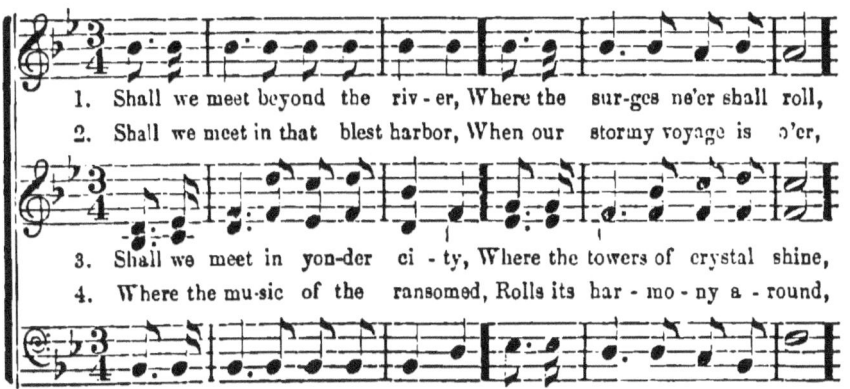

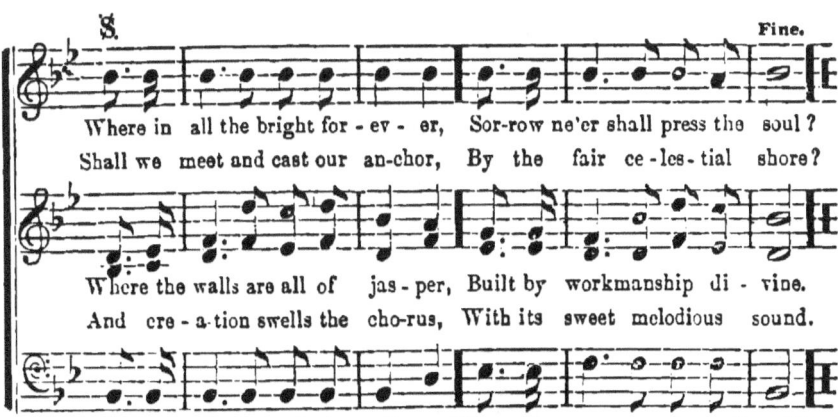

5
Shall we meet with many a loved one,
That was torn from our embrace?
Shall we listen to their voices,
And behold them face to face?
Shall we meet? &c.

6
Shall we meet with Christ our Saviour,
When he comes to claim his own?
Shall we know his blessed favor,
And sit down upon his throne?
Shall we meet? &c.

JESUS OUR FRIEND.

3
Tender and patient, thou,
  Jesus, our heavenly friend;
To thy dear love we bow,
  Jesus our friend.
Oh, in thy spirit pure,
May we our ills endure,
Trusting thy promise sure,
  Jesus our friend.

4
By thy redeeming grace,
  Jesus our heavenly friend;
We hope to see thy face,
  Jesus our friend.
Then will we joyful praise,
Throughout eternal days,
Thy wondrous works and ways
  Jesus our friend.

"I LONG TO BEHOLD HIM." PAUL ARMOND.

1. I long to behold him array'd With glo-ry and light from a-bove:
The King in his beau-ty display'd, His beau-ty of ho-li-est love:
O when shall we meet in the air, And fly to the mountain of God!

2. With him I on Zi-on shall stand, For Je-sus has spoken the word;
The breadth of Im-man-u-el's land Sur-vey by the light of my Lord:
My fullness of rap-ture I find, My heaven of heavens in Thee.

I lan-guish and sigh to be there, Where Jesus has fixed his a-bode.

But when, on thy bo-som reclined, Thy face I am strengthened to see.

How happy the people that dwell
Secure in the city above!
No pain the inhabitants feel,
No sickness or sorrow shall prove.

Physician of souls, unto me
Forgiveness and holiness give;
And then from the body set free,
And then to the city receive.

KIND WORDS. †

1
1 Kind words can never die,
  Cherished and ever blest,
God knows how deep they lie
  Stored in the breast;
Like childhood's simple rhymes,
Said o'er a thousand times,
Go through all lands and climes,
  The heart to cheer.

2
2 Childhood can never die—
  Wrecks of the pleasant past,
Float o'er the memory,
  Bright to the last;
Many a happy thing,
Many a daisy spring
Float o'er time's ceaseless wing,
  Far, far away.

▼ Use small notes first time

3
3 Sweet thoughts can never die,
  Though like the vernal flowers,
Their brightest hues may fly,
  In wintry hours;
But when the gentle dew,
Gives them their charms anew,
With many an added hue
  They bloom again.

4
4 Our souls can never die,
  Though in the silent tomb
Our bodies soon shall lie,
  Wrapt in its gloom;
What though the flesh decay,
Souls pass in peace away,
Live through eternal day
  With Christ above.

† Hymn for tune on the opposite page.

THE WANDERER. S. M.

J. ZUNDEL.

1. I was a wandering sheep, I did not love the fold:
   I did not love my Shepherd's voice, I would not be con-trolled;
   They followed me o'er vale and hill, O'er desert waste and wild:
   I was a wayward child, I did not love my home,
   They found me nigh to death, Famish'd, and faint, and lone;

2. The Shepherd sought his sheep, The Father sought his child;
   I did not love my Father's voice, I loved a-far to roam.
   They bound me with the bands of love, They saved the wand'ring one.

3.
They spoke in tender love,
  They raised my drooping head;
They gently closed my bleeding wounds,
  My fainting soul they fed:
They washed my filth away,
  They made me clean and fair;
They brought me to my home in peace,
  The long sought wanderer.

4.
Jesus my Shepherd is,
  'Twas he that loved my soul,
'Twas he that wash'd me in his blood;
  'Twas he that made me whole:
'Twas he that sought the lost,
  That found the wand'ring sheep:
'Twas he that brought me to the fold;
  'Tis he that still doth keep.

IF WE KNEW.

1. If we knew, while here as pilgrims, What our heavenly joys shall be;
If we knew, what bliss our Saviour, Hath reserved for you and me.

2. If we knew, what crowns are waiting, For the blessed of the Lord;
Would our lips be long-er si-lent, If we knew the blessings stored.

CHORUS.

If we knew, O if we knew, While pilgrims here we roam;
If we knew, O if we knew, While pilgrims here we roam;
If we knew, O if we knew, The heavenly joys to come.
If we knew, O if we knew, The heavenly joys to come.

3
If we knew, when sinners trifle,
  With the spirit's gentlest call;
If we knew, how soon they'd stifle,
  All their better feelings, all.
Cho. If we knew, O if we knew,
  While thoughtless here they roam;
If we knew, O if we knew,
  How near their final doom.

4
If we knew, when death would call them
  From this world they make their choice;
With what pain our hearts would soften,
  If we knew, their hope was lost.
Cho. If we knew, O if we knew,
  While thoughtless here they roam;
If we knew, O if we knew,
  How near their final doom.

YES, WE'LL MEET. 8s & 7s.

(Answer to "Shall we meet.")

1. Yes we'll meet, beyond the ri-ver, When our conflicts all are o'er;
2. Yes we'll meet, in yonder mansions, Where our wand'rings all shall cease,
3. Yes we'll meet, where bliss immortal, Sweeter far than rest can be;
4. Yes we'll meet, where all is onward, Every change new glories bring;

And we'll spend the blest for-ev-er, On that bright ce-les-tial shore.
There we'll meet our dear com-pan-ions, And be crown'd with perfect peace.
And be-fore the throne e-ter-nal, All our earthly triumphs see.
And the host still moving forward, Glo-ri-fy our heavn'ly King.

Hymn for tune on the opposite page.

IF WE KNEW.

If we knew, when walking thoughtless
  Through the crowded, dusty way,
That some pearl of wondrous whiteness
  Close beside our pathway lay,
We would pause where now we hasten,
  We would oft'ner look around,
Lest our careless feet should trample
  Some rare jewel in the ground.
Cho. If we knew, O if we knew,
  While thoughtless here we roam;
If we knew, O if we knew,
  The good there might be done.

2

If we knew what forms were fainting
  For the shade which we should fling,
If we knew what lips were parching
  For the water we should bring,
We would haste with eager footsteps,
We would work with willing hands,
Bearing cooling cups of water,
  Planting rows of shading palms.
  Cho. If we knew, &c.

3

If we knew what feet were weary
  Climbing up the hills of pain,
By the world cast out as evil—
  Poor, repentant Magdalenes—
We no more would dare to scorn them
  With our Pharisaic pride,
Wrapping close our robes around us,
  Passing on the other side.
Cho. If we knew, O if we knew,
  While thoughtless here we roam;
If we knew, O if we knew,
  The good there might be done.

4

If we knew, when friends around us
  Closely press to say "Good bye,"
Which among the lips that kiss us
  First beneath the flowers should lie,
While like rain upon their faces
  Fell our bitter, blinding tears,
Tender words of love eternal
  We would whisper in their ears.
  Cho. If we knew, &c.

THERE, THERE IS REST.

Rev. G. D. BROWNE.

Allegretto.

1. Come poor pil-grim, sad and weary, Why heaves thy breast, Roaming this wide world so
2. There is rest for thee in glo-ry, Among the blest, Lis-ten to the joy-ful
3. There are those who've gone before us, All who are blest, Singing now the hap-py
4. There the golden harps are ringing, Harps of the blest, And the an-gel bands are

CHORUS. Ad Libitum.

dreary, Sighing for rest. Rest, rest, sweet rest.
sto-ry, There, there is rest, Rest, &c.
cho-rus, There, there is rest, Rest, rest, sweet rest.
sing-ing, There, there is rest, Rest, &c.

Where the wick-ed cease from troubling, And the wea-ry are at rest.
Where the wick-ed cease from troubling, And the wea-ry are at rest.

5.
And while we on earth are praying,
Jesus the blest ;
Unto us is sweetly saying
There, there is rest.
Rest, &c.

6.
We shall meet where parting never,
Comes to the blest ;
And we'll safely dwell forever
In heavenly rest.
Rest, &c.

CLAREMONT. 8s & 7s.

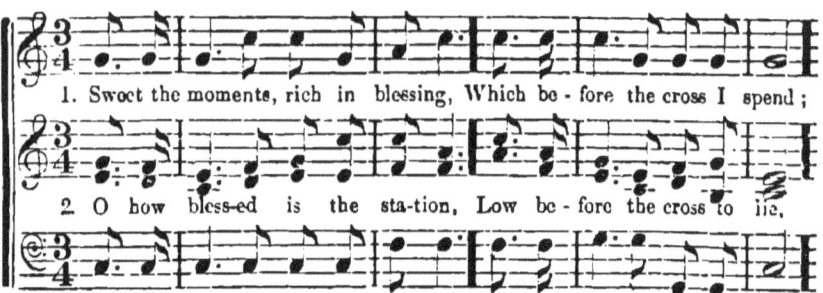

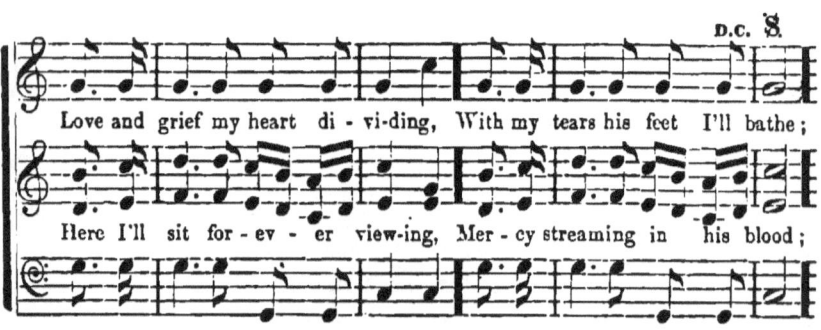

Here it is I find my heaven,
  While upon the Lamb I gaze;
Here I see my sins forgiven,
  Lost in wonder, love and praise.

May I still enjoy this feeling,
  In all need to Jesus go:
Prove each day his blood more healing,
  And himself more deeply know.

EVENING SHADES. 8s & 7s.

D. E. JONES.

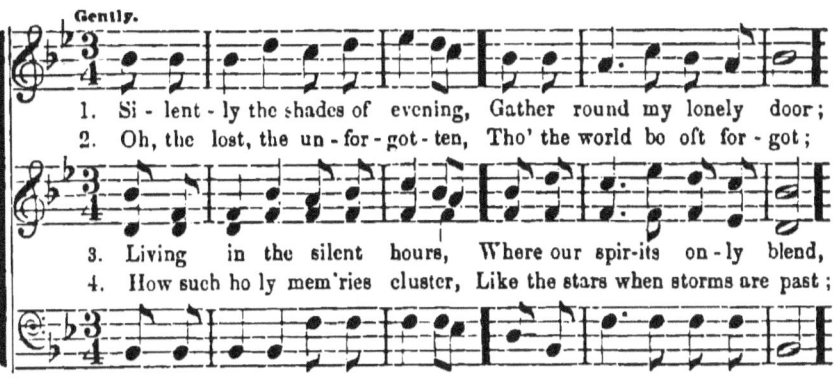

1. Si-lent-ly the shades of evening, Gather round my lonely door;
2. Oh, the lost, the un-for-got-ten, Tho' the world be oft for-got;
3. Living in the silent hours, Where our spir-its on-ly blend,
4. How such ho ly mem'ries cluster, Like the stars when storms are past;

Si-lent-ly they bring be-fore me, Fa-ces I shall see no more.
Oh, the shrouded and the lone-ly! In our hearts they per-ish not.
They, unlink'd with earthly trouble, We still hoping for its end.
Pointing up to that far haven, We may hope to gain at last.

Hymn for Claremont, on the opposite page.

THE NEW CREATION.

1

Love divine, all love excelling,
  Joy of heaven, to earth come down,
Fix in us thy humble dwelling;
  All thy faithful mercies crown.
Jesus, thou art all compassion,—
  Pure unbounded love thou art;
Visit us with thy salvation;
  Enter every trembling heart.

2

Breathe, O breathe thy loving Spirit
  Into every troubled breast;
Let us all in thee inherit;
  Let us find that second rest.
Take away our bent to sinning;
  Alpha and Omega be;
End of faith, as its beginning,
  Set our hearts at liberty.

3

Come, almighty to deliver,
  Let us all thy life receive;
Suddenly return, and never,
  Never more thy temples leave:
Thee we would be always blessing,
  Serve thee as thy hosts above,
Pray, and praise thee without ceasing,
  Glory in thy perfect love.

4

Finish then thy new creation;
  Pure and spotless let us be;
Let us see thy great salvation,
  Perfectly restored in thee:
Changed from glory into glory,
  Till in heaven we take our place,—
Till we cast our crowns before thee,
  Lost in wonder, love, and praise.

JUST AS I AM.

With Energy.

1. Just as I am—without one plea, But that thy blood was shed for me,
2. Just as I am—and waiting not, To rid my soul of one dark blot;

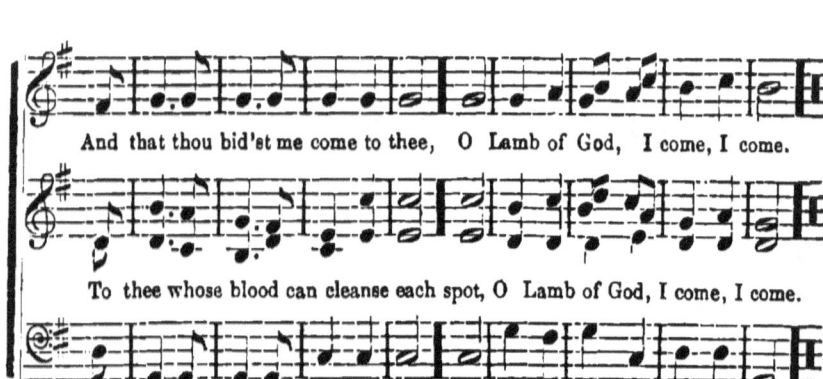

And that thou bid'st me come to thee, O Lamb of God, I come, I come.
To thee whose blood can cleanse each spot, O Lamb of God, I come, I come.

3
Just as I am—poor, wretched, blind ;
Sight, riches, healing of the mind,
Yea, all I need, in thee I find,
    O Lamb of God, I come, I come.

4
Just as I am—though toss'd about,
With many a conflict, many a doubt ;
Fightings within, and fears without—
    O Lamb of God, I come, I come.

5
Just as I am—thou wilt receive,
Wilt welcome, pardon, cleanse, relieve,
Because thy promise I believe—
    O Lamb of God, I come, come.

6
Just as I am—thy love unknown
Has broken every barrier down ;
Now to be thine, yea, thine alone,
    O Lamb of God, I come, I come.

JUST AS THOU ART.

Just as thou art—without one trace
Of love, or joy, or inward grace,
Or meetness for the heavenly place,
    O guilty sinner, come, O come !

2
Thy sins I bore on Calvary's tree ;
The stripes thy due were laid on me,
That peace and pardon might be free—
    O wretched sinner, come, O come !

3
Come, hither bring thy boding fears,
Thy aching heart, thy bursting tears ;
'Tis mercy's voice salutes thine ears :
    O trembling sinner, come, O come !

4
" The Spirit and the bride say, Come ; "
Rejoicing saints re-echo, Come !
Who faints, who thirsts, who will, may come,
    Thy Saviour bids thee, Come, O come !

28. FREEPORT. L. M.

1. Jesus shall reign where'er the sun Does his suc-ces-sive journeys run;
His kingdom spread from shore to shore, Till moons shall wax and wane no more.
2. From north to south the prin-ces meet, To pay their hom-age at his feet;
While western empires own their Lord, And sav-age tribes at-tend his word.
3. To him shall endless prayer be made, And endless prais-es crown his head;
His Name like sweet perfume shall rise With eve-ry morn-ing sac-ri-fice.
4. People and realms of eve-ry tongue Dwell on his love with sweetest song,
And in-fant voic-es shall pro-claim Their ear-ly bless-ings on his name.

29. THE CREATION INVITED TO PRAISE GOD.

1. From all that dwell below the skies,
Let the Creator's praise arise ;
Let the Redeemer's name be sung,
Through every land, by every tongue.

2. Eternal are thy mercies, Lord ;
Eternal truth attends thy word :
Thy praise shall sound from shore to shore,
Till suns shall rise and set no more.

3. Your lofty themes, ye mortals, bring ;
In songs of praise divinely sing ;
The great salvation loud proclaim,
And shout for joy the Saviour's name.

4. In every land begin the song ;
To every land the strains belong :
In cheerful sounds all voices raise,
And fill the world with loudest praise.

O LAND OF REST. C. M.

Arr. for this Work.

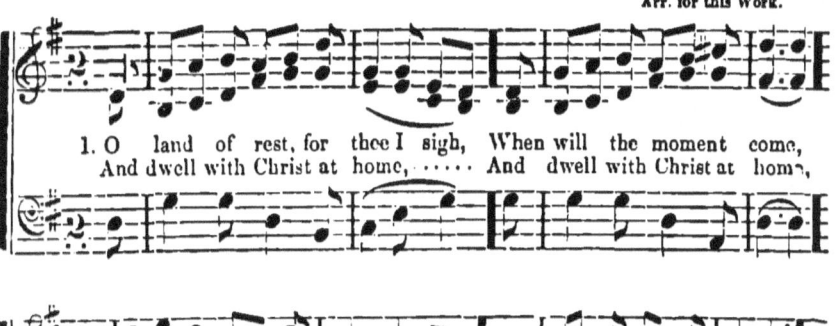

1. O land of rest, for thee I sigh, When will the moment come,
And dwell with Christ at home,...... And dwell with Christ at home,

When I shall lay my ar-mor by, And dwell with Christ at home.
When I shall lay my ar-mor by, And dwell with Christ at home.

2
No tranquil joys on earth I know;
No peaceful sheltering dome:
This world's a wilderness of woe;
This world is not my home.

3
To Jesus Christ I sought for rest,
He bade me cease to roam;
And fly for succor to his breast,
And he'd conduct me home.

4
When, by afflictions sharply tried,
I viewed the gaping tomb;
Although I dread death's chilling flood,
Yet still I sighed for home.

5
Weary of wandering round and round
This vale of sin and gloom,
I long to leave the unhallowed ground,
And dwell with Christ at home.

Conclusion of Hymns for opposite page.

3
A thousand happy guests are there,
In garments white and pure;
'Tis free to all, the rich, the great,
The blind, the maim'd, the poor.
　　Then come to Jesus, &c.

4
Yet there is room, and none depart
Unwelcom'd, unforgiven;
While there is room in Jesus' heart,
There yet is room in heaven.
　　Then come to Jesus, &c.

EXPOSTULATION WITH SINNERS.
Sinners, the voice of God regard;
'Tis mercy speaks to-day;
He calls you, by his sovereign word,
From sin's destructive way.
　　Then come to Jesus, &c.

2
Like the rough sea, that cannot rest,
You live devoid of peace;
A thousand stings within your breast
Deprive your soul of ease.
　　Then come to Jesus, &c.

3
Why will you in the crooked ways
Of sin and folly go?
In pain you travel all your days,
To reap immortal woe.
　　Then come to Jesus, &c.

4
But he who turns to God shall live,
Through his abounding grace;
His mercy will the guilt forgive
Of those who seek his face.
　　Then come to Jesus, &c.

34. MOUNT AUBURN. L. M.

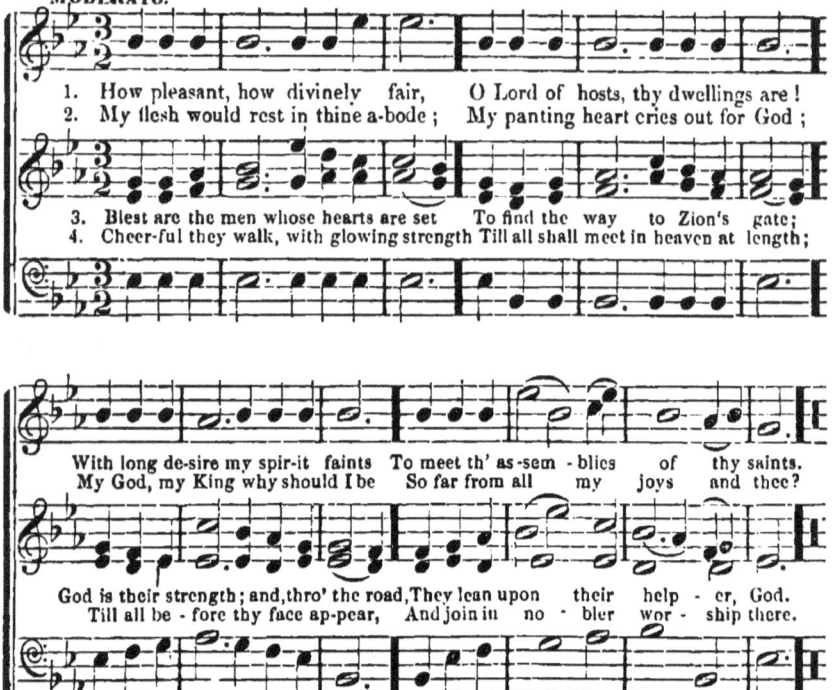

1. How pleasant, how divinely fair, O Lord of hosts, thy dwellings are! With long de-sire my spir-it faints To meet th' as-sem-blies of thy saints.
2. My flesh would rest in thine a-bode; My panting heart cries out for God; God is their strength; and, thro' the road, They lean upon their help-er, God.
3. Blest are the men whose hearts are set To find the way to Zion's gate; My God, my King why should I be So far from all my joys and thee?
4. Cheer-ful they walk, with glowing strength Till all shall meet in heaven at length; Till all be-fore thy face ap-pear, And join in no-bler wor-ship there.

35. LOVE WHICH PASSETH KNOWLEDGE.

1.
Of him who did salvation bring,
I could forever think and sing;
Arise, ye needy,—he'll relieve;
Arise, ye guilty,—he'll forgive.

2.
Ask but his grace, and lo, 'tis given;
Ask, and he turns your hell to heaven:
Though sin and sorrow wound my soul,
Jesus, thy balm will make it whole.

3.
To shame our sins he blush'd in blood;
He closed his eyes to show us God:
Let all the world fall down and know,
That none but God such love can show.

4.
'Tis thee I love, for thee alone
I shed my tears and make my moan;
Where'er I am, where'er I move,
I meet the object of my love.

36. THE HEAVENLY SABBATH.

1.
Another six days' work is done,
Another Sabbath is begun:
Return, my soul, enjoy thy rest,
Improve the day that God hath blest.

2.
Come, bless the Lord, whose love assigns
So sweet a rest to wearied minds;
Draws us away from earth to heaven,
And gives this day the food of seven.

3.
O may our prayers and praises rise
As grateful incense to the skies;
And draw from heaven that sweet repose
Which none but he who feels it knows.

4.
In holy duties may the day,
In holy pleasures pass away;
How sweet a Sabbath thus to spend
In hope of one that ne'er shall end.

37. LEBANON. L. M.

1. Great God, at-tend, while Zi-on sings The joy that from thy presence springs;
2. Might I en-joy the meanest place With-in thy house, O God of grace;
3. God is our sun, he makes our day; God is our shield, he guards our way
4. All need-ful grace will God be-stow, And crown that grace with glory too;

To spend one day with thee on earth Ex-ceeds a thousand days of mirth.
Not tents of ease, or thrones of power, Should tempt my feet to leave thy door.
From all as-saults of hell and sin, From foes with-out, and foes with-in.
He gives us all things, and with-holds No real good from up-right souls.

38.   THE JOY OF THE SABBATH.

1.
Sweet is the work, my God, my King,
To praise thy name, give thanks, and sing;
To show thy love by morning light,
And talk of all thy truth by night.

2.
Sweet is the day of sacred rest;
No mortal cares shall seize my breast;
O may my heart in tune be found,
Like David's harp of solemn sound.

3.
When grace has purified my heart,
Then I shall have a glorious part:
And fresh supplies of joy be shed,
Like holy oil to cheer my head.

4.
Then shall I see, and hear, and know
All I desired or wish'd below;
And every power find sweet employ
In that eternal world of joy.

24. SWEET REST IN HEAVEN.

WM. B. BRADBURY.
From "Cottage Melodies." By permission.

1. As oft we here get wea-ry, And sigh for rest to come; The spir-it saith to cheer us, "There's rest in heaven, thy home;"
   Then let us still press forward, That glorious rest to gain. We'll soon be free from sor-row, From toil, and care, and pain.

2. Loved ones have gone before us, They beckon us a-way, O'er ærial plains they're soar-ing. Blest in e-ter-nal day;
   But we are in the ar-my, And dare not leave our post; We'll fight until we con-quer The foe's most mighty host.

CHORUS.

There is sweet rest in heaven, There is sweet rest in heaven, There is sweet rest, there is sweet rest, There is sweet rest in heaven.

Repeat Chorus softly.

3.
Our Captain's gone before us,
He kindly calls us home
To yonder worlds of glory,
And sweetly bids us come.
The world, the flesh, and Satan,
Will strive to hedge our way,
But we'll o'ercome these powers—
We'll hourly watch and pray.
There is sweet rest, &c.

4.
And Jesus will be with us,
E'en to our journey's end,
In every sore affliction,
His present help to lend.
He never will grow weary,
Though often we request,
He'll give us grace to conquer,
And take us home to rest.
There is sweet rest, &c.

41. FLORENCE. L. M.

Arranged.

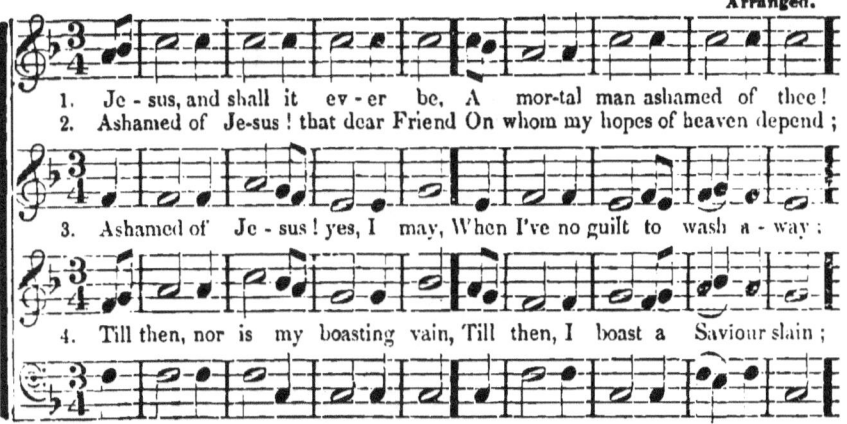

1. Je-sus, and shall it ev-er be, A mor-tal man ashamed of thee!
2. Ashamed of Je-sus! that dear Friend On whom my hopes of heaven depend;
3. Ashamed of Je-sus! yes, I may, When I've no guilt to wash a-way;
4. Till then, nor is my boasting vain, Till then, I boast a Saviour slain;

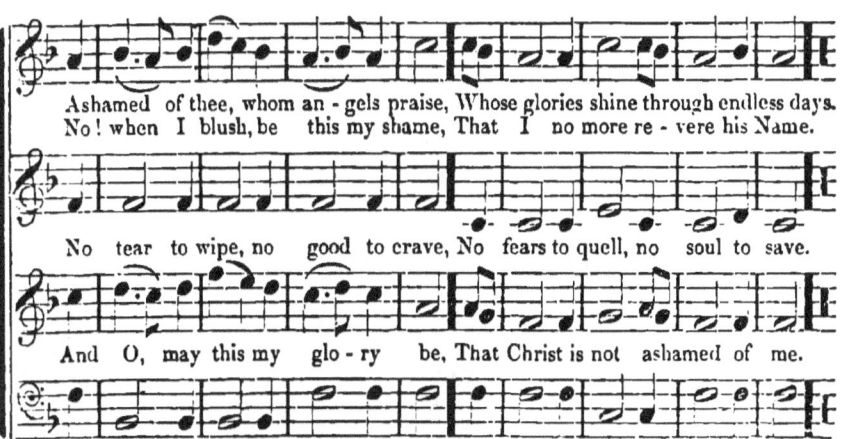

Ashamed of thee, whom an-gels praise, Whose glories shine through endless days.
No! when I blush, be this my shame, That I no more re-vere his Name.
No tear to wipe, no good to crave, No fears to quell, no soul to save.
And O, may this my glo-ry be, That Christ is not ashamed of me.

42. EARTHLY THINGS VAIN AND TRANSITORY.

1.

How vain is all beneath the skies!
   How transient every earthly bliss!
How slender all the fondest ties
   That bind us to a world like this!

2.

The evening cloud, the morning dew,
   The with'ring grass, the fading flower,
Of earthly hopes are emblems true—
   The glory of a passing hour.

3.

But though earth's fairest blossoms die,
   And all beneath the skies is vain,
There is a brighter world on high,
   Beyond the reach of care and pain.

4.

Then let the hope of joys to come
   Dispel our cares, and chase our fears:
If God be ours, we're travelling home,
   Though passing through a vale of tears.

43. CONSOLATION. L. M.

Arranged.

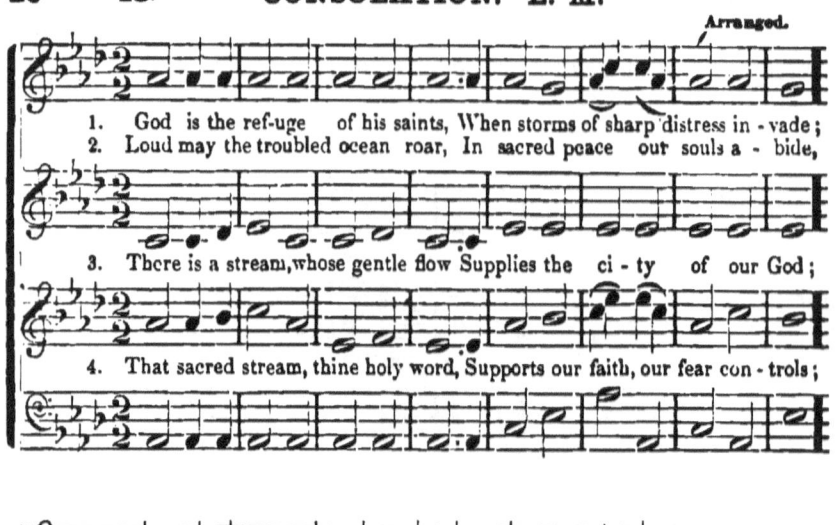

1. God is the refuge of his saints, When storms of sharp distress invade;
Ere we can offer our complaints, Behold him present with his aid.

2. Loud may the troubled ocean roar, In sacred peace our souls abide,
While every nation, every shore, Trembles and dreads the swelling tide.

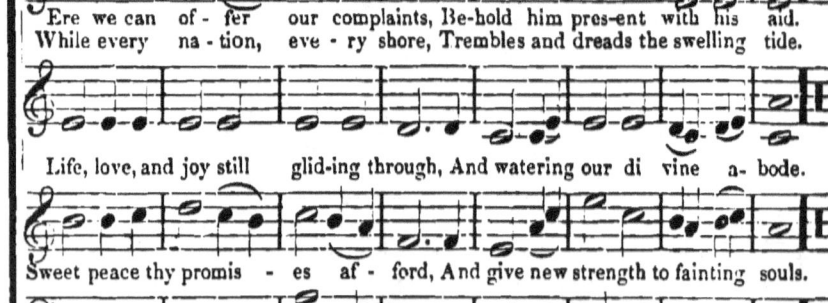

3. There is a stream, whose gentle flow Supplies the city of our God;
Life, love, and joy still gliding through, And watering our divine abode.

4. That sacred stream, thine holy word, Supports our faith, our fear controls;
Sweet peace thy promises afford, And give new strength to fainting souls.

44 MY HEART IS FIXED.

1.
My heart is fix'd on thee, my God;
 I rest my hope on thee alone;
I'll spread thy sacred truths abroad,—
 To all mankind thy love make known

2.
Awake, my tongue; awake, my lyre;
 With morning's earliest dawn arise;
To songs of joy my soul inspire,
 And swell your music to the skies

3.
With those who in thy grace abound,
 To thee I'll raise my thankful voice;
Till every land, the earth around,
 Shall hear, and in thy Name rejoice.

4.
Eternal God, celestial King,
 Exalted be thy glorious Name;
Let hosts in heaven thy praises sing,
 And saints on earth thy love proclaim.

A HOME IN HEAVEN. P. M.

1. A home in heaven! what a joyful thought, As the poor man toils in his weary lot! His heart opprest, and with anguish driven, From his home below, to his home in heaven.

2. A home in heaven! as the sufferer lies On his bed of pain, and uplifts his eyes, To that bright home; what a joy is given, With the blessed thought of his home in heaven.

3.
A home in heaven! when our pleasures fade,
And our wealth and fame in the dust are laid;
And strength decays, and our health is riven,
We are happy still with our home in heaven.

4.
A home in heaven! when our friends are fled
To the cheerless gloom of the mouldering dead;
We wait in hope on the promise given,
To meet them all in our home in heaven.

5.
A home in heaven! when the wheel is broke,
And the golden bowl by the terror-stroke;
When life's bright sun sinks in death's dark even,
We will then fly up to our home in heaven.

6.
Our home in heaven! O, the glorious home!
And the Spirit, joined with the bride, say "Come!"
Come, seek his face, and your sins forgiven,
And rejoice in hope of your home in heaven.

DEFENCE. Concluded.

Safe in-to the ha-ven guide, O re-ceive my soul at last.
False, and full of sin I am; Thou art full of truth and grace.

Cov-er my de-fenceless head With the shad-ow of thy wing.
Spring thou up with-in my heart, Rise to all e-ter-ni-ty.

---

47. WHY WILL YE DIE.

1.
Sinners, turn; why will ye die?
God, your Maker, asks you why?
God, who did your being give,
Made you with himself to live;
He the fatal cause demands;
Asks the work of his own hands,—
Why, ye thankless creatures, why
Will ye cross his love, and die?

2.
Sinners, turn; why will ye die?
God, your Saviour, asks you why?
He, who did your souls retrieve,
Died himself, that ye might live.
Will ye let him die in vain?
Crucify your Lord again?
Why, ye ransom'd sinners, why
Will ye slight his grace, and die?

3.
Sinners, turn; why will ye die?
God, the Spirit, asks you why?
He, who all your lives hath strove,
Urged you to embrace his love.
Will ye not his grace receive?
Will ye still refuse to live?
O ye dying sinners, why,
Why will ye forever die?

48. CHILDREN THE GATE OF HEAVEN.

1.
Little travelers, Zionward,
 Each one entering into rest,
In the kingdom of your Lord,
 In the mansions of the blest;
There, to welcome, Jesus waits,
 Gives the crowns his followers win—
Lift your heads, ye golden gates!
 Let the little travelers in!

2.
Who are they whose little feet,
 Pacing life's dark journey through,
Now have reach'd that heavenly seat,
 They had ever kept in view?
"I from Greenland's frozen land;"
 "I from India's sultry plain;"
"I from Afric's barren sand;"
 "I from islands of the main."

3.
"All our earthly journey past,
 Every tear and pain gone by,
Here together met at last,
 At the portal of the sky!
Each the welcome 'COME' awaits,
 Conquerors over death and sin!"—
Lift your heads, ye golden gates!
 Let the little travelers in!

4.
Death itself shall then be vanquish'd,
And its sting shall be withdrawn;
Shout for gladness, O ye ransomed,
Hail with joy the rising morn.
  Cho. There is rest, &c.

5.
Sing, O sing, ye heirs of glory:
Shout your triumph as you go;
Zion's gates will open for you,
You shall find an entrance through.
  Cho. There is rest, &c.

3.

O! to grace how great a debtor
Daily I'm constrain'd to be!
Let thy goodness, like a fetter,
Bind my wand'ring heart to thee:

Prone to wander, Lord, I feel it—
Prone to leave the God I love;
Here's my heart, O take and seal it;
Seal it for thy courts above.

"THERE'S NOT A STAR." C. M.

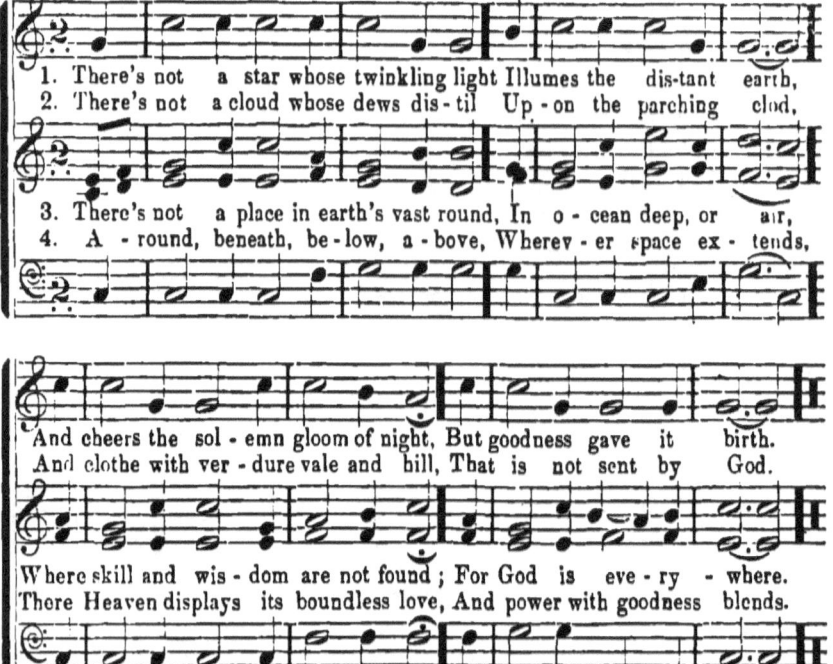

1. There's not a star whose twinkling light Illumes the distant earth, And cheers the solemn gloom of night, But goodness gave it birth.
2. There's not a cloud whose dews distil Upon the parching clod, And clothe with verdure vale and hill, That is not sent by God.
3. There's not a place in earth's vast round, In ocean deep, or air, Where skill and wisdom are not found; For God is everywhere.
4. Around, beneath, below, above, Wherever space extends, There Heaven displays its boundless love, And power with goodness blends.

52. HEAVENLY REST IN ANTICIPATION.

1.
When I can read my title clear
 To mansions in the skies,
I'll bid farewell to every fear,
 And wipe my weeping eyes.

2.
Should earth against my soul engage,
 And fiery darts be hurl'd,
Then I can smile at Satan's rage,
 And face a frowning world.

3.
Let cares like a wild deluge come,
 Let storms of sorrow fall,—
So I but safely reach my home,
 My God, my heaven, my all.

4.
There I shall bathe my weary soul
 In seas of heavenly rest,
And not a wave of trouble roll
 Across my peaceful breast.

53. LOVE FOR THE SUNDAY SCHOOL.

1.
I love the Sabbath school—the place
 My youthful feet have trod,
Where I have heard of wisdom's ways,
 That lead to peace with God.

2.
I love the Sabbath-school,—'tis there
 The praise of God we sing,—
'Tis there we bow the knee in prayer
 To God, our heavenly King.

3.
I love the Sabbath-school—where we
 The Holy Bible read,—
Which tells of Christ, who came to be
 A Saviour in our need.

4.
O, that when life's few cares are past
 Our teachers we may meet
Upon the blissful plains, and cast
 Our crowns at Jesus' feet.

54. EDEN IS MY HOME. C. M.

1. Oh! I have roamed thro' sin's dark maze, A stranger to delight;
Not friendship's hopes nor love's sweet smiles, Could make my pathway bright,
Till on the sky a star arose, And lit night's sable dome:
To that fair land my spirit flies, And angels bid me come:

2. O! Eden, is my place of rest, I long to reach its shore;
To throw these troubles from my breast, To weep and sigh no more:
O, steer my bark by that sweet star, For Eden is my home.
O, steer my bark o'er Jordan's waves, For Eden is my home.

3.
O take me from this world of woe,
To my blest home above,
Where tears of sorrow never flow,
And all the air is love:
There happy spirits wait for me,
And Jesus bids me come:
O, steer my bark to that fair land,
For Eden is my home.

55. THE PILGRIM'S SONG. 7s.

Arranged.

1. Children of the beavenly King, As ye jour-ney, sweet-ly sing:
Sing your Saviour's wor-thy praise, Glorious in his works and ways.
2. Ye are travelling home to God, In the way the fa-thers trod:
Je-sus Christ, God's on-ly Son, Bids you un-dis-mayed go on.
3. Fear not, brethren, joy-ful stand, On the bor-ders of your land:
They are hap-py now, and ye Soon their hap-pi-ness shall see.
4. Lord, sub-mis-sive make us go, Glad-ly leav-ing all be-low:
On-ly thou our Lead-er be, And we still will fol-low thee.

56. GOD'S PEOPLE.

1.
People of the living God,
 I have sought the world around,
Paths of sin and and sorrow trod,
 Peace and comfort nowhere found.

2.
Now to you my spirit turns,
 Turns, a fugitive unblessed ;
Brethren, where your altar burns,
 O receive me into rest !

3.
Lonely I no longer roam,
 Like the cloud, the wind, the wave ;
Where you dwell shall be my home,
 Where you die shall be my grave ;

4.
Mine the God whom you adore,
 Your Redeemer shall be mine ;
Earth can fill my heart no more,
 Every idol I resign.

57. DANGER OF DELAY.

1.
Haste, O sinner ; now be wise ;
 Stay not for the morrow's sun :
Wisdom if you still despise,
 Harder is it to be won.

2.
Haste, and mercy now implore ;
 Stay not for the morrow's sun,
Lest thy season should be o'er,
 Ere this evening's stage be run.

3.
Haste, O sinner ; now return ;
 Stay not for the morrow's sun,
Lest thy lamp should cease to burn
 Ere salvation's work is done.

4.
Haste, O sinner ; now be blest ;
 Stay not for the morrow's sun,
Lest perdition thee arrest,
 Ere the morrow is begun.

THE HILL OF ZION. S. M. 35

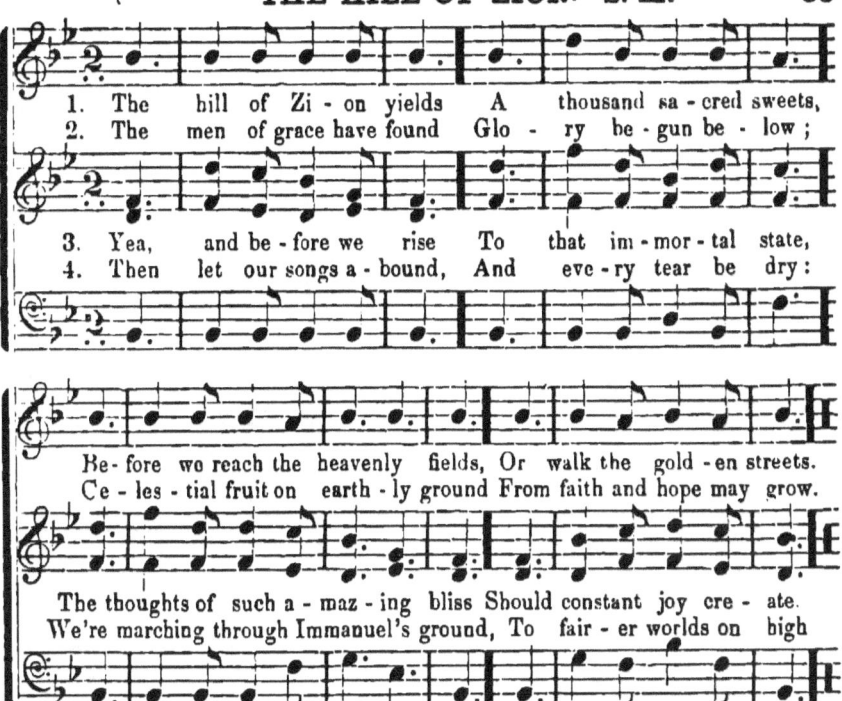

1. The hill of Zi-on yields A thousand sa-cred sweets,
2. The men of grace have found Glo-ry be-gun be-low;
3. Yea, and be-fore we rise To that im-mor-tal state,
4. Then let our songs a-bound, And eve-ry tear be dry:

Be-fore we reach the heavenly fields, Or walk the gold-en streets.
Ce-les-tial fruit on earth-ly ground From faith and hope may grow.
The thoughts of such a-maz-ing bliss Should constant joy cre-ate.
We're marching through Immanuel's ground, To fair-er worlds on high

59. GLORY BEGUN BELOW.

1.
Come, ye that love the Lord,
 And let your joys be known;
Join in a song with sweet accord,
 While ye surround his throne.

2.
Let those refuse to sing
 Who never knew our God,
But servants of the heavenly King
 May speak their joys abroad.

3.
There we shall see his face,
 And never, never sin;
There, from the rivers of his grace,
 Drink endless pleasures in:

4.
Yea, and before we rise
 To that immortal state,
The thoughts of such amazing bliss
 Should constant joys create.

60. FOR DILIGENCE AND WATCHFULNESS.

1.
A charge to keep I have,
 A God to glorify;
A never-dying soul to save,
 And fit it for the sky.

2.
To serve the present age,
 My calling to fulfil,—
O may it all my powers engage,
 To do my Master's will.

3.
Arm me with jealous care,
 As in thy sight to live;
And O, thy servant, Lord, prepare,
 A strict account to give.

4.
Help me to watch and pray,
 And on thyself rely,
Assured, if I my trust betray,
 I shall forever die.

61. LONG TIME AGO. 8s & 4s.

Arranged.

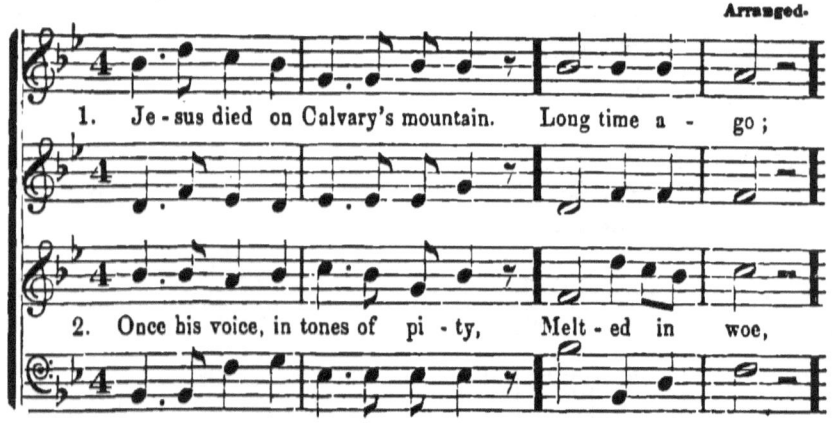

1. Jesus died on Calvary's mountain. Long time ago;
2. Once his voice, in tones of pity, Melted in woe,

And salvation's rolling fountain Now freely flows.
And he wept o'er Judah's city, Long time ago.

3.
On his head the dews of midnight, Fell long ago;
Now a crown of dazzling sunlight Sits on his brow

4.
Jesus died, yet lives in heaven, No more to die;
Bleeding Jesus, blessed Saviour, Now reigns on high.

5.
Now in heaven he's interceding For dying man,
Soon he'll finish all his pleading, And come again,

6.
When he comes, a voice from heav'n Shall pierce the tomb,
"Come, ye blessed of my Father, Children, come home."

3. Each saint has a mansion prepared and all
    furnished,
  Ere from this clay house he is summoned
    to move;
  Its gates and its towers with glory are burnished;
  O say, will you go to the Eden above?
  Will you go, &c.

4. And yet, guilty sinner, we would not forsake thee,
  We halt yet a moment as onward we move;
  O come to thy Lord, in his arms he will take thee,
  And bear thee along to the Eden above.
  Will you go, &c.

63. HOMEWARD BOUND.

C. S. HARRINGTON.

1. Out on an ocean all boundless we ride, We're homeward bound, homeward bound.
Toss'd on the waves of a rough restless tide, We're, &c.
Promise of which on us each he bestowed, We're, &c.

2. Wildly the storm sweeps us on as it roars, We're homeward bound, homeward bound.
Look! yonder lie the bright heavenly shores, We're, &c.
O, how we fly 'neath the loud-creaking sail, We're, &c.

Far from the safe, quiet harbor we've rode, Seeking our Father's celestial abode.

Steady, O pilot! stand firm at the wheel, Steady! we soon shall outweather the gale.

3.
We live as pilgrims and strangers below,
   We're homeward bound;
'Though often tempted, yet onward we go,
   We're homeward bound.
Trials and croses we cheerfully bear,
Toils and temptation expecting to share,
We hasten forward, content with the fare,
   We're homeward bound.

4.
We'll tell the world, as we journey along,
   We're homeward bound;
Try to persuade them to enter our throng,
   We're homeward bound.
Come, trembling sinner, forlorn and opprest
Join in our number, O come and be blest,
Journey with us to the mansion of rest,
   We're homeward bound.

64. HEAVENWARD BOUND.

In life's bright morning the tempest we brave,
   We're heav'nward bound,
Out on the dark, and the storm-broken wave,
   We're heavenward bound.
Earth's bright attraction grow dim in the light,
The far distant city reveals to our sight,
Toward which we're urging our unceasing flight,
   We're heavenward bound.

2.
Now to the youthful the voyage we commend,
   Come, with us go, with us go;
Welcome! a welcome to *all* we extend,
   Say, will you go, will you go?
Swiftly! O swiftly! fly! fly to the ark!
Our ship now is passing,—make haste to embark!
The night hastens quickly, all dreary and dark,
   Haste! let us go, let us go!

65. "I'M GOING HOME." L. M.

Oct. 8, 1859.

1. I have a home be-yond the sky, Where saints in glo-ry never die;
CHORUS. I'm going home; in that fair land, To join a hap-py, sinless band,

2. In that fair land there still is room, Where weary pilgrims may get home;
CHORUS. I'm go-ing home; in that fair land, To join a hap-py, sinless band,

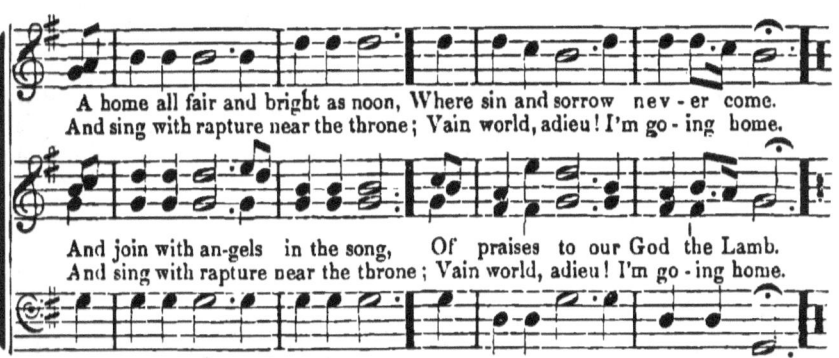

A home all fair and bright as noon, Where sin and sorrow nev-er come.
And sing with rapture near the throne; Vain world, adieu! I'm go-ing home.

And join with an-gels in the song, Of praises to our God the Lamb.
And sing with rapture near the throne; Vain world, adieu! I'm go-ing home.

3.
When done with earth; its follies past,
I'll reach my father-land at last;
To sit and sing around the throne,
Glory to God; I'm safe at home.
CHORUS.
When safe at home, in that fair land,
I'll join the happy, sinless band,
And sing with rapture near the throne,
Vain world, adieu! I'm safe at home.

66. LOVING—KINDNESS.

1.
Awake, my soul, in joyful lays,
And sing thy great Redeemer's praise;
He justly claims a song from thee,—
His loving-kindness, O! how free!
CHORUS.
His loving-kindness, has prepared
A heavenly mansion with my Lord,
He justly claims a song from me,
His loving-kindness, O! how free!

2 When trouble, like a gloomy cloud,
Has gathered thick, and thundered loud,
He near my soul has always stood,—
His loving-kindness, O how good!
His loving-kindness, &c.

3 Often I feel my sinful heart
Prone from my Saviour to depart,
But though I oft have him forgot,
His loving-kindness changes not.
His loving-kindness, &c.

4 Soon shall I pass the gloomy vale,
Soon all my mortal powers must fail;
O! may my last expiring breath
His loving-kindness sing in death.
His loving kindness, &c.

5 Then let me mount and soar away
To the bright world of endless day,
And sing with rapture and surprise
His loving-kindness in the skies.
His loving-kindness, &c.

68. MORNING HYMN.

1 This morning, Lord, attend,
   While we are bow'd in prayer;
   And from thy glorious throne descend,
   And in our midst appear.

2 Make this thy dwelling-place,
   While we assemble stay,
   Inspire each youthful soul with grace,
   And wash our sins away.

3 O let this morning be
   Devoted to thy ways;
   And consecrate our school to thee,
   And fill each heart with praise.

4 To child and teacher, Lord,
   Be thy best favours given;
   And may we all, with one accord,
   Make sure our way to heaven.

69. I DO BELIEVE. C. M.

Arranged.

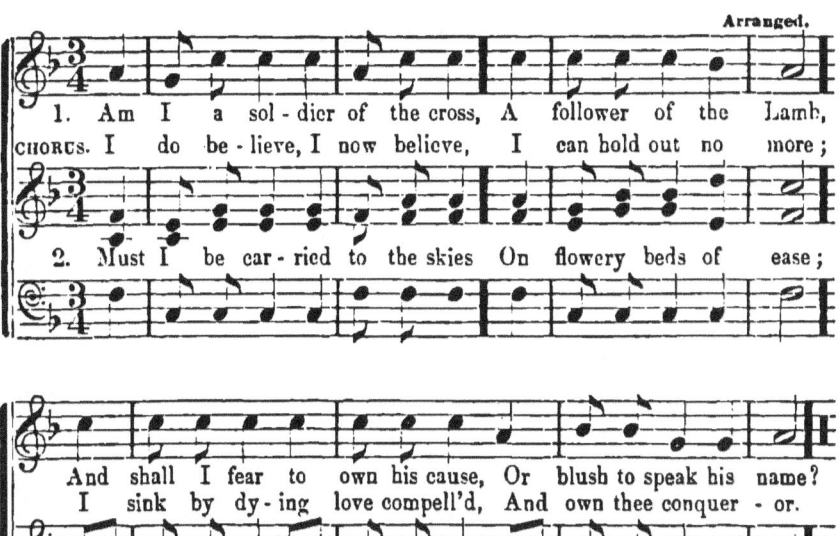

1. Am I a sol-dier of the cross, A follower of the Lamb,
And shall I fear to own his cause, Or blush to speak his name?

CHORUS. I do be-lieve, I now believe, I can hold out no more;
I sink by dy-ing love compell'd, And own thee conquer-or.

2. Must I be car-ried to the skies On flowery beds of ease;
While oth-ers fought to win the prize, And sail'd through bloody seas?

3.
Are there no foes for me to face?
Must I not stem the flood?
Is this vile world a friend to grace,
To help me on to God?

4.
Since I must fight if I would reign,
Increase my courage, Lord;
I'll bear the toil, endure the pain,
Supported by thy word.

5.
Thy saints in all this glorious war,
Shall conquer, though they die:
They see the triumph from afar,—
By faith they bring it nigh.

6.
When that illustrious day shall rise,
And all thy armies shine
In robes of vict'ry through the skies,
The glory shall be thine.

70. EFFICACY OF THE ATONING BLOOD.

1.
There is a fountain fill'd with blood,
Drawn from Immanuel's veins;
And sinners, plunged beneath that flood,
Lose all their guilty stains.

2.
The dying thief rejoiced to see
That fountain in his day;
And there may I, though vile as he,
Wash all my sins away.

3.
Thou dying Lamb! thy precious blood
Shall never lose its power,
Till all the ransom'd Church of God
Are saved, to sin no more.

4.
E'er since, by faith, I saw the stream
Thy flowing wounds supply,
Redeeming love has been my theme,
And shall be, till I die.

71. THE SINNER'S INVITATION.

Arranged from The Wesleyan Harp.

1. Sinner go, will you go, to the highlands of heaven? Where the storms never blow, And the long summer's given. And the deep-laden boughs Of life's fair tree are bending, Where the bright blooming flowers Are their odors emitting, And where life's crystal stream Is unceasingly flowing,

2. Where the rich golden fruit in bright clusters are pending, And the leaves of the bowers, In the breezes are flitting. And the verdure is green, And eternally growing,

3.
Where the saints robed in white,
  Cleaned in life's flowing fountain,
Shining beauteous and bright,
  Shall inhabit the mountain.
Where no sin nor dismay,
  Neither trouble nor sorrow
Shall be felt, for a day,
  Nor be feared for the morrow.

4.
He's prepared thee a home;
  Sinner, canst thou believe it?
And invites thee to come;
  Sinner, wilt thou receive it?
O come, sinner, come,
  For the tide is receding,
And the Saviour will soon,
  And forever cease pleading.

2.

My gracious Master, and my God,
　Assist me to proclaim,—
To spread, through all the earth abroad,
　The honours of thy Name.

3.

Jesus! the Name that charms our fears,
　That bids our sorrows cease;
'Tis music in the sinner's ears,
　'Tis life, and health, and peace.

4.

He breaks the power of cancell'd sin,
　He sets the pris'ner free;
His blood can make the foulest clean;
　His blood avail'd for me.

5.

He speaks, and, list'ning to his voice,
　New life the dead receive;
The mournful, broken hearts rejoice;
　The humble poor believe.

73. TURNER. C. M.

MAXIM.

1. Come, Holy Spirit, heavenly Dove, With all thy quick'ning powers; Kindle a flame of sacred love, In these cold hearts of ours.

2
Look how we grovel here below,
   Fond of these earthly toys;
Our souls, how heavily they go,
   To reach eternal joys.

3
In vain we tune our formal songs,—
   In vain we strive to rise;
Hosannas languish on our tongues,
   And our devotion dies.

4
Father, and shall we ever live
   At this poor dying rate;
Our love so faint, so cold to thee,
   And thine to us so great.

5
Come, Holy Spirit, heavenly Dove,
   With all thy quick'ning powers;
Come, shed abroad a Saviour's love,
   And that shall kindle ours.

74. I WOULD NOT LIVE ALWAY. 11s.

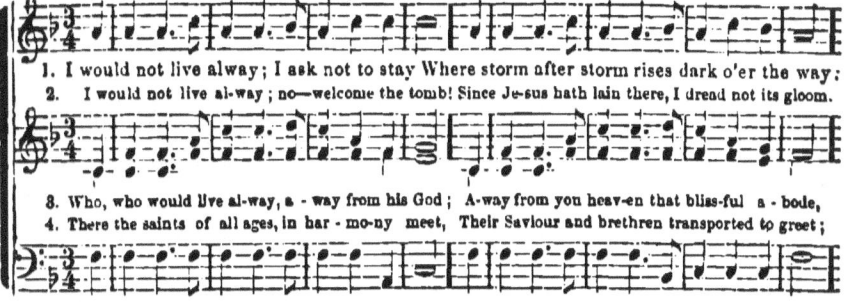

1. I would not live alway; I ask not to stay Where storm after storm rises dark o'er the way;
2. I would not live al-way; no—welcome the tomb! Since Je-sus hath lain there, I dread not its gloom.
3. Who, who would live al-way, a-way from his God; A-way from you heav-en that bliss-ful a-bode,
4. There the saints of all ages, in har-mo-ny meet, Their Saviour and brethren transported to greet;

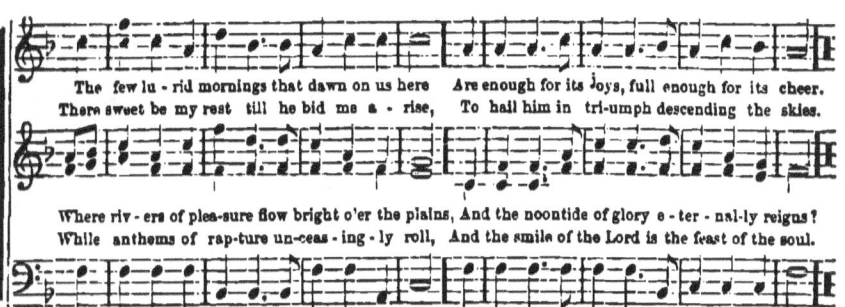

The few lu-rid mornings that dawn on us here Are enough for its joys, full enough for its cheer.
There sweet be my rest till he bid me a-rise, To hail him in tri-umph descending the skies.
Where riv-ers of plea-sure flow bright o'er the plains, And the noontide of glory e-ter-nal-ly reigns?
While anthems of rap-ture un-ceas-ing-ly roll, And the smile of the Lord is the feast of the soul.

75. JESUS THE SAVIOUR.

1 O Jesus, my Saviour, to thee I submit;
With love and thanksgiving fall down at thy feet;
In sacrifice offer my soul, flesh and blood;
Thou art my Redeemer who brought me to God.

2 I love thee, I love thee, I love thee, my Lord;
I love thee, my Saviour, I love thee, my God:
I love thee, I love thee, and that thou dost know,
But how much I love thee, I never can show.

3 I'm happy, I'm happy, O wondrous account!
My joys are immortal, I stand on the mount!
I gaze on my treasure, and long to be there,
With Jesus and angels, my kindred so dear.

4 O Jesus, my Saviour with thee I am blest!
My life and salvation, my joy and my rest!
Thy name be my theme, and thy love be my song,
Thy grace shall inspire both my heart and my tongue.

5 O who's like my Saviour? He's Salem's bright King;
He smiles, and he loves me, and learns me to sing;
I'll praise him, I'll praise him, with notes loud and shrill,
While rivers of pleasure my spirit doth fill.

76. THE BIBLE, THE WORD OF TRUTH.

1 The Bible — the Bible! more precious than gold,
The hopes and the glories its pages unfold;
It speaks of salvation—wide opens the door—
Its offers are free to the rich and the poor.

2 The Bible—the Bible! blest volume of truth,
How sweetly it smiles on the season of youth;
It bids us seek early the "Pearl of great price,"
Ere the heart is enslaved in the bondage of vice.

3 The Bible—the Bible! the valleys shall ring,
And hill-tops re-echo the notes that we sing;
Our banners inscribed with its precepts and rules,
Shall long wave in triumph, the joy of our schools.

MEET AGAIN. 7s.

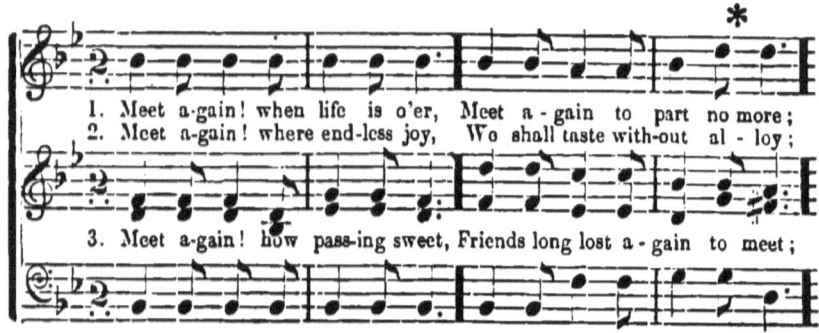

1. Meet a-gain! when life is o'er, Meet a-gain to part no more;
2. Meet a-gain! where end-less joy, We shall taste with-out al-loy;
3. Meet a-gain! how pass-ing sweet, Friends long lost a-gain to meet;

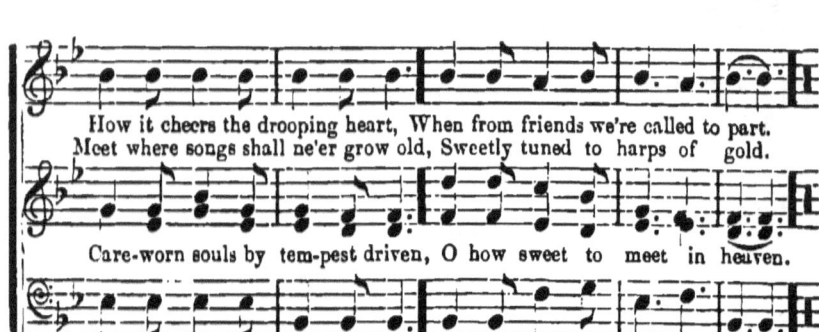

How it cheers the drooping heart, When from friends we're called to part.
Meet where songs shall ne'er grow old, Sweetly tuned to harps of gold.
Care-worn souls by tem-pest driven, O how sweet to meet in heaven.

HYMN FOR AN INFANT SCHOOL.

First Class.
Little schoolmates, can you tell,
Who has kept us safe and well,
Through the watches of the night,
Brought us safe to see the light?

2   *Second Class.*
Yes; it is our God does keep
Little children while they sleep;
He has kept us safe from harm,
Shelter'd by his powerful arm.

3   *First Class.*
Can you tell who gives us food,
Clothes, and home, and parents good,
Schoolmates dear, and teachers kind,
Useful books, and active mind?

4   *Second Class.*
Yes; our heavenly Father's care
Gives us all we eat and wear;
All our books, and all our friends,
God, in kindness, to us sends.

5   *Chorus.*
O, then, let us thankful be,
For his mercies large and free;
Every morning let us raise
Our young voices in his praise.

Tune on 49th page.
I want to be an angel,
  And with the angels stand,
A crown upon my forehead,
  A harp within my hand;
There, right before my Saviour,
  So glorious and bright,
I'll make the sweetest music,
  And praise him day and night.

2
I know I'm weak and sinful,
  But Jesus will forgive;
For many little children
  Have gone to heaven to live.
Dear Saviour, when I languish,
  And lay me down to die,
O send a shining angel,
  To bear me to the sky.

3
Oh, there I'll be an angel,
  And with the angels stand,
A crown upon my forehead,
  A harp within my hand;
And there, before my Saviour,
  So glorious and bright,
I'll join the heavenly music,
  And praise him day and night.

"O WHEN SHALL I SEE JESUS." 7s & 6s.

DR. LARDNER.

1. O when shall I see Jesus, And reign with him above?
And from that flowing fountain, Drink everlasting love?

2. But now I am a soldier, My Captain's gone before,
He's given me my orders, And bids me not give o'er.

When shall I be delivered From this vain world of sin,
If I continue faithful, A righteous crown he'll give,

Use small notes first time.

And with my blessed Jesus, Drink endless pleasures in.
And all his valiant soldiers Eternal life shall have.

3
Through grace I am determined
To conquer though I die!
And then away to Jesus
On wings of love I'll fly:
Farewell to sin and sorrow,
I bid you all adieu;
And O, my friends, prove faithful,
And on your way pursue.

4
And if you meet with troubles
And trials on your way,
Then cast your cares on Jesus,
And don't forget to pray;
Gird on the heavenly armor
Of faith, and hope, and love,
And when the combat's ended
He'll carry you above.

THE ANGELS ARE CALLING. 7s & 6s.

Then when the day is closing,
The weary will have rest,
The mourners cease to languish,
Peace reign in every breast:

And I, my labors finished
On earth, no more shall roam,
For angels who are calling,
Will take me to their home.

REST IN HEAVEN. 6s, or S. M.

1. Should sorrow o'er thy brow, Its darkened shadows fling,—
And hopes that cheer thee now, Die in their early spring;
And gladness cease to beam Upon its clouded day,
There's rest, there's rest, There's rest for thee in Heaven.

2. If ever life should seem To thee a toilsome way,—
Should pleasure at its birth, Fade like the hues of even,
If, like the weary dove, O'er shoreless oceans driven,
Turn thou away from earth, There's rest for thee in heaven.
Raise thou thine eyes above, There's rest for thee in heaven.

Coda. May be omitted.

3 But O! if thornless flowers,
  Throughout thy pathway bloom,—
And joy'ly fleet the hours,
  Unstained by earthly gloom;—
Still, let not ev'ry thought
  To this poor world be given;
Nor always be forgot,
  Thy better rest in Heaven.

4 When sickness pales thy cheek,
  And dims thy lustrous eye,
And pulses low and weak,
  Tell of a time to die;—
Sweet hope will whisper then,
  "Though thou from earth be riven,
There's bliss beyond the ken,
  There's rest for thee in Heaven."

REST IN HEAVEN. Concluded.

O turn from earth a-way, There's rest for thee in Heaven.
O turn from earth a-way, There's rest for thee in Heaven.

24. THE SECOND DEATH.

1 O where shall rest be found.—
Rest for the weary soul ?
'Twere vain the ocean's depths to sound,
Or pierce to either pole.

2 The world can never give
The bliss for which we sigh ;
'Tis not the whole of life to live,
Nor all of death to die.

3 Beyond this vale of tears
There is a life above,
Unmeasured by the flight of years ;
And all that life is love.

4 There is a death, whose pang
Outlasts the fleeting breath :
O what eternal horrors hang
Around the second death !

5 Thou God of truth and grace !
Teach us that death to shun ;
Lest we be banished from thy face,
Forever more undone.

25. ACCEPTING THE INVITATION.

1 Come, weary sinners, come,
Groaning beneath your load ;
The Saviour calls his wanderers home,
Hast to your pard'ning God.

2 Come, all by guilt oppress'd,
Answer the Saviour's call—
O come, and I will give you rest,
And I will save you all.

3 Redeemer, full of love,
We would thy word obey,
And all thy faithful mercies prove :
O take our guilt away.

4 We would on thee rely ;
On thee would cast our care ;
Now to thine arms of mercy fly,
And find salvation there.

26. THE GOODLY LAND.

1 Far from these scenes of night,
Unbounded glories rise,
And realms of joy and pure delight,
Unknown to mortal eyes.

2 Fair land !—could mortal eyes
But half its charms explore,
How would our spirits long to rise,
And dwell on earth no more !

3 No cloud those regions know,—
Realms ever bright and fair ;
For sin, the source of mortal wo,
Can never enter there.

4 O may the prospect fire
Our hearts with ardent love,
Till wings of faith, and strong desire,
Bear every thought above.

5 Prepared, by grace divine,
For thy bright courts on high,
Lord, bid our spirits rise and join
The chorus of the sky.

THE PRODIGAL'S RETURN. C. M.

1. Af-flictions tho' they seem severe, In mercy oft are sent, They stopp'd the prodigal's career, And caus'd him to repent.

2. What have I gained by sin, he said, But hunger, shame and fear? My Father's house abounds with bread, While I am starving here.

3. I'll go and tell him all I've done, Fall down before his face, Unworthy to be called his son, I'll seek a servant's place.

   D.C. My Father's house has large supplies, And bounteous are his hands.

I'll die no more for bread, he cried, Nor starve in foreign lands;
I'll die no more for bread, he cried, Nor starve in foreign lands;

4. His Father saw him coming back,
   He saw, and ran, and smiled,
   And threw his arms around the neck
   Of his rebellious child.
       I'll die no more, &c.

5. Father, I've sinned, but O forgive!
   Enough! the Father said;
   Rejoice, my house, my Son's alive,
   For whom I mourn'd as dead.
       I'll die no more, &c.

6. Now let the fatted calf be slain,
   And spread the news around;
   My son was dead, and lives again;
   Was lost, but now is found.
       I'll die no more, &c.

7. 'Tis thus the Lord his love reveals,
   To call poor sinners home,
   More than a Father's love he feels,
   And welcomes all that come.
       I'll die no more, &c.

COMING HOME. C. M.

A. D. MERRILL.

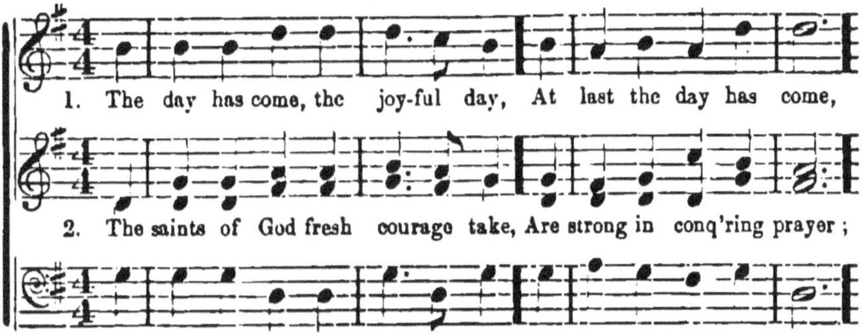
1. The day has come, the joy-ful day, At last the day has come,
2. The saints of God fresh courage take, Are strong in conq'ring prayer ;

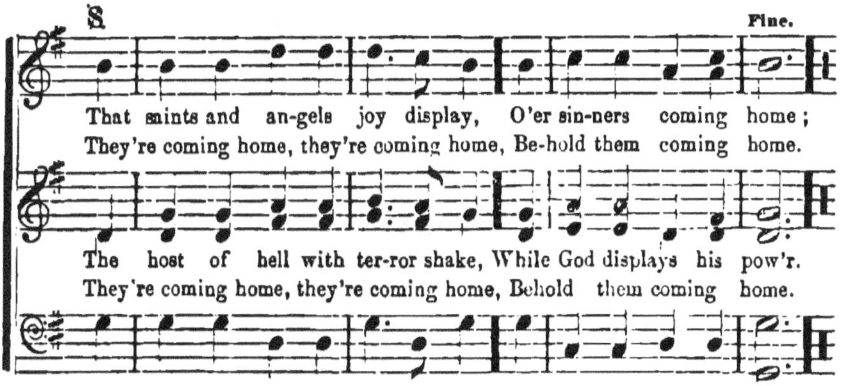
Fine.
That saints and an-gels joy display, O'er sin-ners coming home ;
They're coming home, they're coming home, Be-hold them coming home.
The host of hell with ter-ror shake, While God displays his pow'r.
They're coming home, they're coming home, Behold them coming home.

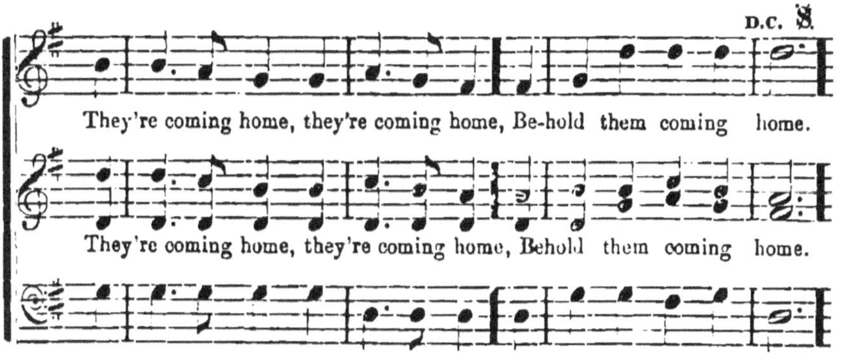
D.C.
They're coming home, they're coming home, Be-hold them coming home.
They're coming home, they're coming home, Behold them coming home.

3

To all the regions round about,
The news has swiftly flown,
That sinners, deep in guilt, have sought
And found what others spurn.

4

Back-sliders, too, begin to view
What traitors they have been ;
Confessing, ask, "what shall I do ?"
A hell I feel within

CROSS AND CROWN. C. M.
Western Melody.

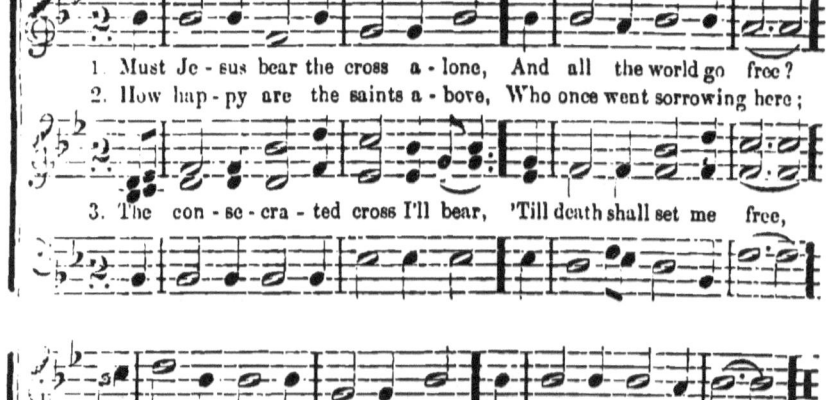

1. Must Jesus bear the cross alone, And all the world go free? No, there's a cross for every one, And there's a cross for me.
2. How happy are the saints above, Who once went sorrowing here; But now they taste unmingled love, And joy without a tear.
3. The consecrated cross I'll bear, 'Till death shall set me free, And then go home my crown to wear, For there's a crown for me.

NOT ASHAMED OF THE GOSPEL.

1.
I'm not ashamed to own my Lord,
Or to defend his cause;
Maintain the honor of his word,—
The glory of his cross.

2.
Jesus, my God!—I know his name;
His name is all my trust:
Nor will he put my soul to shame,
Nor let my hope be lost.

3.
Firm as his throne his promise stands,
And he can well secure
What I've committed to his hands,
Till the decisive hour.

4.
Then will he own my worthless name
Before his Father's face,
And in the New Jerusalem
Appoint my soul a place.

THE LAMB WORSHIPPED.

1.
Come, let us join our cheerful songs
With angels round the throne:
Ten thousand thousand are their tongues,
But all their joys are one.

2.
Worthy the Lamb that died, they cry,
To be exalted thus:
Worthy the Lamb, our hearts reply,
For he was slain for us.

3.
Jesus is worthy to receive
Honour and power divine;
And blessings more than we can give,
Be, Lord, forever thine.

4.
The whole creation join in one,
To bless the sacred name
Of him that sits upon the throne,
And to adore the Lamb.

EXHORTATION. C. M.   57

2. O the transporting, rapturous scene,
   That rises to my sight!
   Sweet fields arrayed in living green,
   And rivers of delight.

3. O'er all those wide-extended plains
   Shines one eternal day;
   There God, the Son, forever reigns,
   And scatters night away.

4. No chilling winds, or pois'nous breath,
   Can reach that healthful shore;
   Sickness and sorrow, pain and death,
   Are felt and feared no more.

5. Fill'd with delight, my raptured soul,
   Would here no longer stay:
   Though Jordan's waves around me roll,
   Fearless I'd launch away.

EMMONS. C. M.

Arranged from BURGMULLER.

1. Thou dear Redeemer, dying Lamb, We love to hear of thee,
2. Oh, may I ever hear thy voice In mercy to me speak;
3. While Jesus shall be still my theme, While on this earth I stay;
4. When I appear in yonder cloud, With all his favored throng,

No music's like thy charming name, Nor half so sweet can be.
In thee, my priest, will I rejoice, And thy salvation seek,
I'll sing my Jesus' lovely name, When all things else decay,
Then will I sing more sweet, more loud, And Christ shall be my song,

THE PRECIOUS NAME.

How sweet the name of Jesus sounds
   In a believer's ear;
It soothes his sorrows, heals his wounds,
   And drives away his fear.

2.
It makes the wounded spirit whole,
   And calms the troubled breast;
'Tis manna to the hungry soul,
   And to the weary, rest.

3.
Dear Name, the rock on which I build,
   My shield and hiding place;
My never-failing treasure, filled
   With boundless stores of grace.

4.
Jesus, my Shepherd, Saviour, Friend,
   My Prophet, Priest, and King,
My Lord, my Life, my Way, my End,
   Accept the praise I bring.

5.
I would thy boundless love proclaim
   With every fleeting breath;
So shall the music of thy name
   Refresh my soul in death.

MARLOW. C. M.

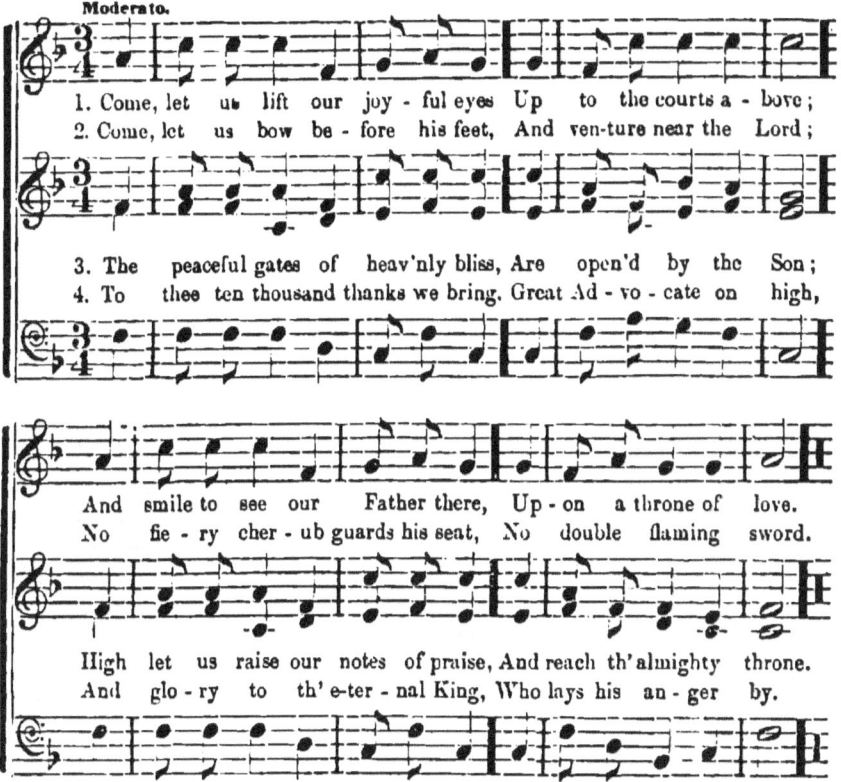

1. Come, let us lift our joyful eyes Up to the courts above;
And smile to see our Father there, Upon a throne of love.
High let us raise our notes of praise, And reach th' almighty throne.

2. Come, let us bow before his feet, And venture near the Lord;

3. The peaceful gates of heav'nly bliss, Are open'd by the Son;
No fiery cherub guards his seat, No double flaming sword.

4. To thee ten thousand thanks we bring, Great Advocate on high,
And glory to th' eternal King, Who lays his anger by.

GRATEFUL REMEMBRANCE.

According to thy gracious word,
  In meek humility,
This will I do, my dying Lord,—
  I will remember thee.

2
Thy body, broken for my sake,
  My bread from heaven shall be:
Thy testamental cup I take,
  And thus remember thee.

3
When to the cross I turn mine eyes,
  And rest on Calvary,
O Lamb of God, my Sacrifice,
  I must remember thee!

4
Remember thee and all thy pains,
  And all thy love to me;
Yea, while a breath, a pulse remains,
  Will I remember thee.

THE DREADFUL SENTENCE.

That awful day will surely come,
  Th' appointed hour makes haste,
When I must stand before my Judge,
  And pass the solemn test.

2
Jesus, thou source of all my joys,
  Thou ruler of my heart,
How could I bear to hear thy voice
  Pronounce the word,—Depart!

3
What, to be banish'd from my Lord,
  And yet forbid to die;
To linger in eternal pain,
  And death forever fly?—

4
O, wretched state of deep despair,
  To see my God remove,
And fix my doleful station where
  I must not taste his love.

DUNDEE. C. M.

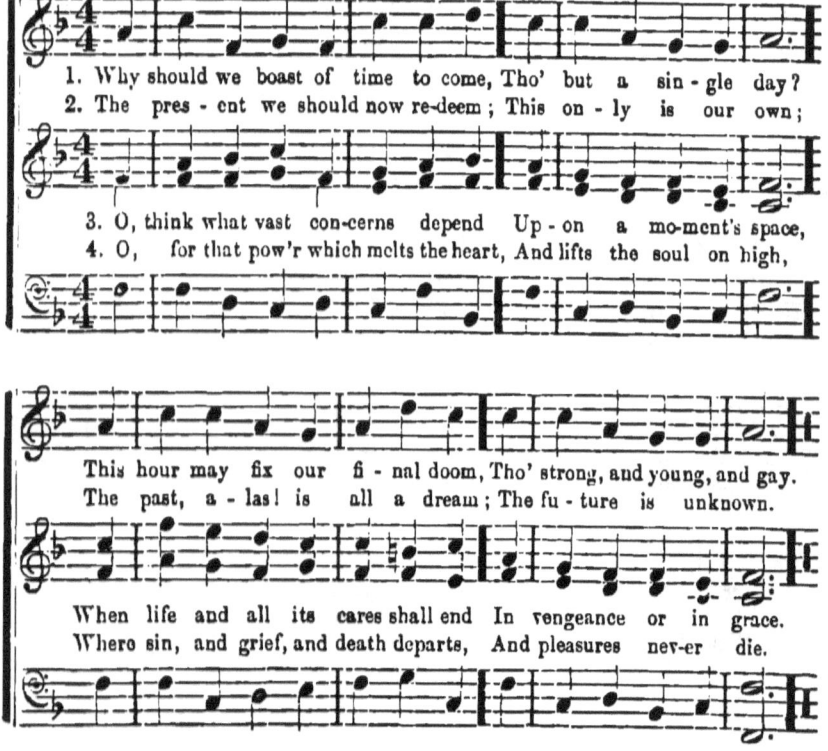

1. Why should we boast of time to come, Tho' but a single day?
2. The present we should now redeem; This only is our own;
3. O, think what vast concerns depend Upon a moment's space,
4. O, for that pow'r which melts the heart, And lifts the soul on high,

This hour may fix our final doom, Tho' strong, and young, and gay.
The past, alas! is all a dream; The future is unknown.
When life and all its cares shall end In vengeance or in grace.
Where sin, and grief, and death departs, And pleasures never die.

GODLY SORROW AT THE CROSS.

Alas! and did my Saviour bleed?
And did my Sov'reign die?
Would he devote that sacred head
For such a worm as I?

2
Was it for crimes that I have done,
He groan'd upon the tree?
Amazing pity! grace unknown!
And love beyond degree!

3
Well might the sun in darkness hide,
And shut his glories in,
When Christ, the mighty Maker, died,
For man, the creature's sin.

4
But drops of grief can ne'er repay
The debt of love I owe:
Here, Lord, I give myself away,—
'Tis all that I can do.

SIN KILLS BEYOND THE TOMB.

Vain man, thy fond pursuits forbear;
Repent, thine end is nigh;
Death, at the farthest, can't be far:
O think, before thou die.

2
Reflect, thou hast a soul to save;
Thy sins, how high they mount!
What are thy hopes beyond the grave?
How stands that dark account?

3
Death enters, and there's no defence,
His time there's none can tell;
He'll in a moment call thee hence,
To heaven, or down to hell,

4
Thy flesh, (perhaps thy greatest care)
Shall into dust consume;
But, ah! destruction stops not there;
Sin kills beyond the tomb.

PHILLIPS. C. M.   F. HUNTEN. Arranged.

1. When the worn spirit wants repose, And sighs her God to seek,
How sweet to hail the evening's close, That ends the weary week!
Breathe, heav'nly spirit, source of peace, A sabbath o'er my soul.

2. How sweet to hail the early dawn, That opens on the sight,
When first that soul-reviving morn, Sheds forth new rays of light!

3. Sweet day! thine hours too soon will cease; Yet, while they gently roll,

4. When will my pilgrimage be done, The world's long week be o'er,
That sabbath dawn, which needs no sun, That day which fades no more?

REMEMBERING CHRIST.

If human kindness meets return,
  And owns the grateful tie;—
If tender thoughts within us burn
  To feel a friend is nigh;—

2
O, shall not warmer accents tell
  The gratitude we owe
To Him who died our fears to quell,
  And save from endless woe?

3
While yet his anguish'd soul survey'd
  Those pangs he would not flee,
What love his latest words displayed!—
  "Meet, and remember me."

4
Remember thee! thy death, thy shame,
  The griefs which thou didst bear!
O memory, leave no other name
  But his recorded there.

"TO DIE IS GAIN."

Why should our tears in sorrow flow,
  When God recalls his own;
And bids them leave a world of woe,
  For an immortal crown?

2
Is not e'en death a gain to those
  Whose life to God was given?
Gladly to earth their eyes they close
  To open them in heaven.

3
Their toils are past—their work is done,
  And they are fully blest;
They fought the fight, the victory won,
  And entered into rest.

4
Then let our sorrows cease to flow,—
  God has has recalled his own;
But let our hearts, in every wo,
  Still say,—"Thy will be done?",

PETERBORO'. C. M.
English Tune.

1. How sweet, how heavenly is the sight, When those who love the Lord,
In one anoth-er's peace de-light, And so ful-fil his word.

2. O! may we feel each brother's sigh, And with him bear a part;
May sor-row flow from eye to eye, And joy from heart to heart.

3. Let love, in one de-light-ful stream, Through ev'ry bosom flow;
And u-nion sweet, and dear esteem, In ev-'ry ac-tion glow.

4. Love is the gold-en chain that binds The hap-py souls a-bove;
And he's an heir to heaven that finds His bo-som glow with love.

FOLLOWING DEPARTED WORTHIES.

Give me the wings of faith, to rise
Within the veil, and see
The saints above, how great their joys,
How bright their glories be.

2

Once they were mourning here below,
And bathed their couch with tears;
They wrestled hard, as we do now,
With sins, and doubts, and fears.

3

I ask them whence their victory came;
They, with united breath,
Ascribe their conquest to the Lamb,
Their triumph to his death.

4

They marked the footsteps that he trod;
His zeal inspired their breast;
And, following their incarnate God,
Possessed the promised rest.

PRAYER IN SCHOOL.

When in the Sabbath School we pray
As we are taught to do,
God will not answer what we say,
Unless we feel it too.

2

Yet foolish thoughts our hearts beguile,
And, when we pray or sing,
We're often thinking, all the while,
About some other thing.

3

O, let us never, never dare
To act the trifler's part,
Or think that God will hear a prayer
That comes not from the heart!

4

But if we make his ways our choice
As holy children do,
Then, while we seek him with our voice
Our hearts will love him too.

BALERMA. C. M.

Old Scottish Melody.

1. God moves in a mys-te-rious way, His wonders to perform;
2. Deep in un-fath-om-a-ble mines Of nev-er-fail-ing skill,
3. Ye fear-ful saints fresh courage take; The clouds ye so much dread
4. Judge not the Lord by fee-ble sense, But trust him for his grace;

He plants his footsteps in the sea, And rides up-on the storm.
He treasures up his bright designs, And works his sovereign will.
Are big with mer-cy, and shall break, In blessings on your head.
Be-hind a frowning prov-i-dence, He hides a smiling face.

5
His purposes will ripen fast,
 Unfolding every hour:
The bud may have a bitter taste,
 But sweet will be the flower,

6
Blind unbelief is sure to err,
 And scan his works in vain :
God is his own interpreter,
 And he will make it plain.

GRATEFUL ACKNOWLEDGMENTS.

I love the Lord ; he heard my cries,
 And pitied every groan :
Long as I live, when troubles rise,
 I'll hasten to his throne.

2
I love the Lord; he bow'd his ear,
 And chased my grief away :
O let my heart no more despair,
 While I have breath to pray.

3
The Lord beheld me sore distress'd,
 He bade my pains remove :
Return, my soul, to God thy rest,
 For thou hast known his love.

THE REQUEST.

Father, whate'er of earthly bliss
 Thy sovereign will denies,
Accepted at thy throne of grace
 Let this petition rise :—

2
" Give me a calm, a thankful heart,
 From every murmur free;
The blessings of thy grace impart,
 And let me live to thee.

3
Oh, let the hope that thou art mine,
 My life and death attend—
Thy presence through my journey shine,
 And crown my journey's end.

DISCIPLE. 8s & 7s.

Arr. for this work.

1. Je-sus, I my cross have tak-en, All to leave and fol-low thee.
2. Let the world despise and leave me; They have left my Saviour too;

Nak-ed, poor, despised, for-sak-en, Thou from hence my all shalt be;
Yet how rich is my con-dition! God and heav'n are still my own.

Human hearts and looks deceive me—Thou art not like them un-true.
Foes may hate, and friends disown me—Show thy face and all is bright.

Per-ish eve-ry fond am-bi-tion, All I've sought, or hoped, or known.
And while thou shalt smile up-on me, God of wis-dom, love, and might;

REJOICING IN HOPE.

1. Know, my soul, thy full salvation;
Rise o'er sin, and fear, and care;
Joy to find in every station,
Something still to do or bear:
Think what Spirit dwells within thee;
Think what Father's smiles are thine;
Think what Jesus did to win thee:
Child of heaven, canst thou repine?

2. Haste thee on from grace to glory,
Armed by faith and winged by prayer;
Heaven's eternal day's before thee;
God's own hand shall guide thee there:
Soon shall close thy earthly mission;
Soon shall pass thy pilgrim days;
Hope shall change to glad fruition,
Faith to sight, and prayer to praise.

THE SHIP OF CANAAN. 8s & 7s.

Rev. G. W. BALOU,
By Permission.

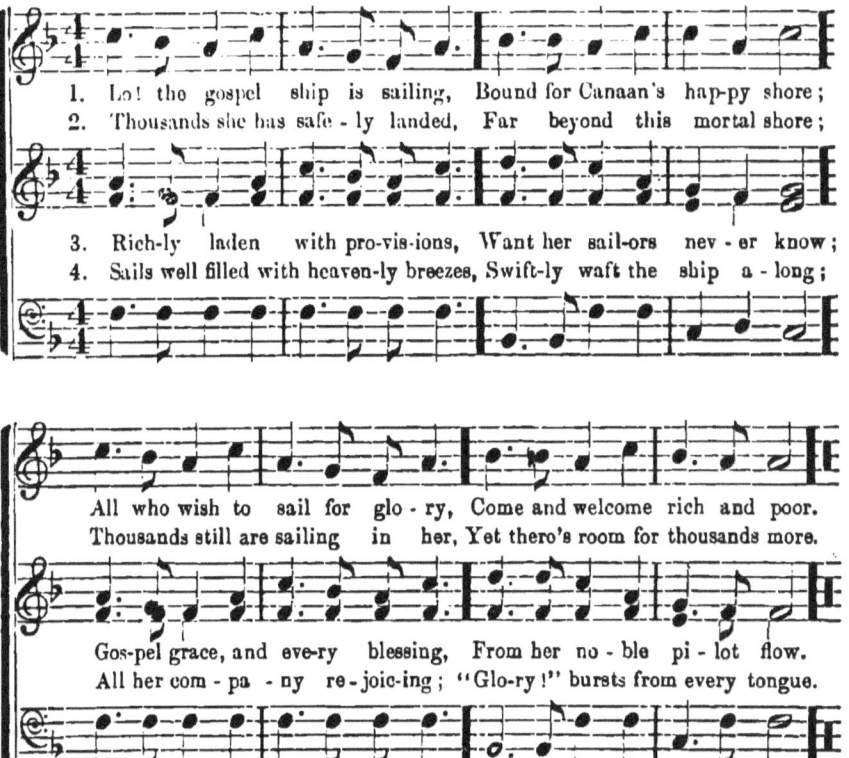

1. Lo! the gospel ship is sailing, Bound for Canaan's hap-py shore;
2. Thousands she has safe-ly landed, Far beyond this mortal shore;
3. Rich-ly laden with pro-vis-ions, Want her sail-ors nev-er know;
4. Sails well filled with heaven-ly breezes, Swift-ly waft the ship a-long;

All who wish to sail for glo-ry, Come and welcome rich and poor.
Thousands still are sailing in her, Yet there's room for thousands more.
Gos-pel grace, and eve-ry blessing, From her no-ble pi-lot flow.
All her com-pa-ny re-joic-ing; "Glo-ry!" bursts from every tongue.

SAILOR'S SONG.

Tossed upon life's raging billow,
 Sweet it is, O Lord, to know,
Thou didst press a sailor's pillow,
 And canst feel a sailor's woe.

2

And though loud the wind is howling,
 Fierce though flash the lightnings red,
Darkly though the storm-cloud's scowling
 O'er the sailor's anxious head—

3

Thou canst calm the raging ocean,
 All its noise and tumult still,
Hush the tempest's wild commotion,
 At the bidding of thy will.

4

Thus my heart the hope will cherish,
 While to thee I lift mine eye,
Thou wilt save me ere I perish,
 Thou wilt hear the sailor's cry.

AUTUMN.

See the leaves around us falling,
 Dry and withered to the ground,
Thus to thoughtless mortals calling,
 In a sad and solemn sound—

2

"Youth, on length of days presuming,
 Who the paths of pleasure tread,
View us, late in beauty blooming,
 Numbered now among the dead."

3

"What though yet no losses grieve you,
 Gay with health and many a grace;
Let not cloudless skies deceive you;
 Summer gives to Autumn place.

4

On the tree of life eternal
 Let our highest hopes be stayed:
This alone, forever vernal,
 Bears a leaf that shall not fade.

63 "THE MELLOW EVE IS GLIDING." 7s & 6s.

"THE MELLOW EVE IS GLIDING." Concluded.

May an-gels round me sing-ing, Thus hymn my last re-pose.
O! on the last bright morning, May I in glo-ry wake.

10. THE UNIVERSAL ANTHEM. P. M.

1 When shall the voice of singing
　Flow joyfully along?
When hill and valley ringing
　With one triumphant song,
Proclaim the contest ended,
　And Him who once was slain,
Again to earth descended,
　In righteousness to reign.

2 Then from the craggy mountains
　The sacred shout shall fly;
And shady vales and fountains
　Shall echo the reply.
High tower and lowly dwelling
　Shall send the chorus round,
All hallelujahs swelling
　In one eternal sound!

11. DEPARTING MISSIONARIES. P. M.

1 Roll on, thou mighty ocean;
　And, as thy billows flow,
Bear messengers of mercy
　To every land below.
Arise, ye gales, and waft them
　Safe to the destined shore;
That man may sit in darkness,
　And death's black shade no more.

2 O thou eternal Ruler,
　Who holdest in thine arm
The tempests of the ocean,
　Protect them from all harm!
Thy presence, Lord, be with them,
　Wherever they may be;
Though far from us who love them,
　Still let them be with thee.

12. THE CRY OF THE HEATHEN. P.M.

1 From Greenland's icy mountains,
　From India's coral strand;
Where Afric's sunny fountains
　Roll down their golden sand;
From many an ancient river,
　From many a palmy plain,
They call us to deliver
　Their land from error's chain.

2 What though the spicy breezes
　Blow soft o'er Ceylon's isle;
Though every prospect pleases,
　And only man is vile:
In vain with lavish kindness
　The gifts of God are strown;
The heathen in his blindness
　Bows down to wood and stone.

3 Shall we, whose souls are lighted
　With wisdom from on high,
Shall we to men benighted
　The lamp of life deny?
Salvation!—O salvation!
　The joyful sound proclaim,
Till earth's remotest nation
　Has learned Messiah's name.

4 Waft, waft ye winds, his story,
　And you, ye waters roll,
Till, like a sea of glory,
　It spreads from pole to pole:
Till o'er our ransom'd nature
　The Lamb for sinners slain,
Redeemer, King, Creator,
　In bliss returns to reign.

"O 'TIS DELIGHT." C. M.

1. O 'tis de-light with-out al-loy, Jesus to hear thy name:
   My spir-it leaps with in-ward joy; I feel the sa-cred flame.
   And sound from eve-ry joy-ful string Through all the realms of bliss.
   My pas-sions hold a pleasing reign, When love inspires my breast,

2. This is the grace must live and sing, When faith and hope shall cease.
   Love, the di-vin-est of the train, The sov'-reign of the rest.
   I leap to meet thy kind em-brace, I come, O Lord, I come.
   Swift I as-cend the heavenly place, And has-ten to my home,

18 FAITH SEES THE FINAL TRIUMPH.

1. Am I a soldier of the cross,—
    A foll'wer of the Lamb,—
    And shall I fear to own his cause,
      Or blush to speak his name?

2. Must I be carried to the skies
    On flowery beds of ease;
    While others fought to win the prize,
      And sail'd through bloody seas?

3. Are there no foes for me to face?
    Must I not stem the flood?
    Is this vile world a friend to grace,
      To help me on to God?

4. Since I must fight if I would reign,
    Increase my courage, Lord;
    I'll bear the toil, endure the pain,
      Supported by thy word.

5. Thy saints in all this glorious war
    Shall conquer, though they die:
    They see the triumph from afar,—
      By faith they bring it nigh.

6. When that illustrious day shall rise,
    And all thy armies shine
    In robes of vict'ry through the skies,
      The glory shall be thine.

WOODLAND. 8s & 6s. or C. M.

N. D. GOULD.

Moderato.

1. I love to steal a-while a-way From eve-ry cumb'ring care,
2. I love in sol-i-tude to shed The pen-i-ten-tial tear,
3. I love to think on mercies past, And fu-ture good im-plore,—
4. I love by faith to take a view Of brighter scenes in heaven;

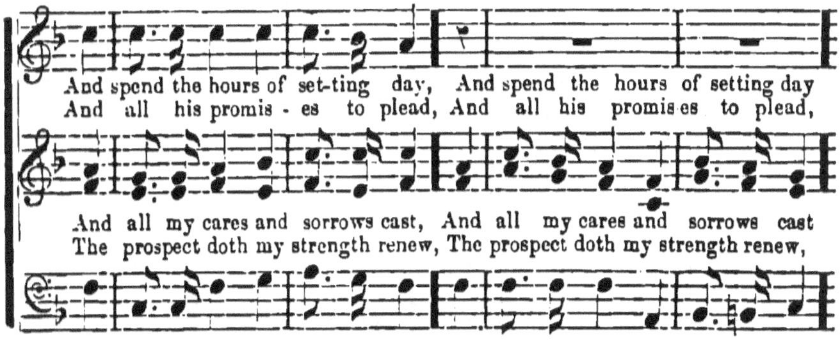

And spend the hours of set-ting day, And spend the hours of setting day
And all his promis-es to plead, And all his promises to plead,
And all my cares and sorrows cast, And all my cares and sorrows cast
The prospect doth my strength renew, The prospect doth my strength renew,

In humble, grateful prayer.
Where none but God can hear.
On him whom I a-dore.
While here by tempest driven.

5
Thus, when life's toilsome day is o'er,
May its departing ray
Be calm as this impressive hour,
And lead to endless day.

THE LAND OF REST.

There is an hour of peaceful rest,
  To mourning wand'rers given;
There is a joy for souls distress'd,
A balm for every wounded breast,—
'Tis found above in heaven.

2
There is a home for weary souls
  By sin and sorrow driven,
When toss'd on life's tempestuous shoals,
Where storms arise and ocean rolls,
  And all is drear but heaven.

3
There faith lifts up the tearless eye,
  To brighter prospects given;
And views the tempest passing by,
The evening shadows quickly fly,
  And all serene in heaven.

4
There fragrant flowers immortal bloom,
  And joys supreme are given;
There rays divine disperse the gloom;
Beyond the confines of the tomb
  Appears the dawn of heaven.

"WHO ARE THESE IN BRIGHT ARRAY."

E. IVES.
Arr. for this Work.

1. Who are these in bright ar-ray, This ex-ult-ing, hap-py throng,
Round the al-tar night and day, Hymning one tri-umphant song?
Now, be-fore the throne of God, Sealed with his al-migh-ty name:
Worthy is the lamb, once slain, Blessing, hon-or, glo-ry, power,
Clad in raiment pure and white, Vic-tor palms in eve-ry hand:

2. These through fiery tri-als trod; These from great af-flictions came;
Wis-dom, rich-es to ob-tain, New do-min-ion eve-ry hour.
Thro' their great Redeemer's might, More than con-quer-ors they stand.

3.
Hunger, thirst, disease, unknown,
On immortal fruits they feed;
Them the Lamb, amidst the throne,
Shall to living fountains lead:

Joy and gladness banish sighs;
Perfect love dispels all fears;
And forever from their eyes
God shall wipe away their tears.

3
Now incline me to repent ;
Let me now my sins lament;
Now my soul revolt deplore ;
Weep, believe, and sin no more ;
God is love! &c.

4
There for me the Saviour stands ;
Shows his wounds, and spreads his hands ;
God is love! I know, I feel ;
Jesus weeps, and loves me still ;
God is love! &c.

1. Praise to God, im-mor-tal praise, For the love that crowns our days; Bounteous source of ev'-ry joy, Let thy praise our tongues em-ploy.
2. All that Spring, with bounteous hand, Scatter'd o'er the smiling land; All that lib-'ral autumn pours From his rich, o'er-flow-ing stores.
3. These, to that dear source we owe, Whence our sweetest comforts flow; These, thro' all my hap-py days, Claim my cheerful songs of praise.
4. Lord, to thee my soul should raise Grateful, never-end-ing praise; And, when ev-'ry blessing's flown, Love thee for thy-self a-lone.

GRATITUDE AND SUPPLICATION.

Thou that dost my life prolong,
Kindly aid my morning song;
Thankful, from my couch I rise,
To the God that rules the skies.

2

Thou hast kept me through the night;
'Twas thy hand restored the light:
Lord, thy mercies still are new,
Plenteous as the morning dew.

3

Still my feet are prone to stray;
O, preserve me through the day:
Dangers every where abound;
Sins and snares beset me round.

4

Gently, with the dawning ray,
On my soul thy beams display;
Sweeter than the smiling morn,
Let thy cheering light return.

SABBATH EVENING.

Softly fades the twilight ray
Of the holy Sabbath day;
Gently as life's setting sun,
When the Christian's course is run.

2

Night her solemn mantle spreads
O'er the earth, as daylight fades;
All things tell of calm repose,
At the holy Sabbath's close.

3

Peace is on the world abroad;
'Tis the holy peace of God,—
Symbol of the peace within,
When the spirit rests from sin.

4

Saviour, may our Sabbaths be
Days of peace and joy in thee,
Till in heaven our souls repose,
Where the Sabbath ne'er shall close.

PLEYEL'S HYMN. 7s.

PLEYEL. 73

1. Lord of hosts, how lovely fair, E'en on earth thy temples are!
2. From thy gracious presence flows Bliss that softens all our woes;
3. Here, we sup-pli-cate thy throne; Here, thy pard'ning grace is known:

Here thy waiting peo-ple see, Much of heaven, and much of thee.
While thy Spirit's ho-ly fire Warms our hearts with pure desire.
Here we learn thy righteous ways—Taste thy love and sing thy praise.

A BLESSING HUMBLY REQUESTED.

Lord, we come before thee now;
At thy feet we humbly bow;
O, do not our suit disdain;
Shall we seek thee, Lord, in vain?

2

Lord, on thee our souls depend;
In compassion now descend;
Fill our hearts with thy rich grace;
Tune our lips to sing thy praise.

3

Comfort those who weep and mourn;
Let the time of joy return;
Those that are cast down, lift up;
Make them strong in faith and hope.

4

Grant that all may seek and find
Thee a God supremely kind,
Heal the sick; the captive free;
Let us all rejoice in thee.

PRAYER FOR THE SALVATION OF CHILDREN.

God of mercy, hear our prayer
For the children thou hast given;
Let them all thy blessings share—
Grace on earth, and bliss in heaven.

2

In the morning of their days
May their hearts be drawn to thee;
Let them learn to lisp thy praise
In their earliest infancy.

3

When we see their passions rise,
Sinful habits unsubdued,
Then to thee we lift our eyes,
That their hearts may be renewed.

4

Cleanse their souls from every stain,
Through the Saviour's precious blood;
Let them all be born again,
And be reconciled to God.

SICILY. 8s, 7s & 4s.

1. Lord, dismiss us with thy blessing; Fill our hearts with joy and peace;
2. Thanks we give, and adoration, For thy gospel's joyful sound;

Let us each, thy love possessing, Triumph in redeeming grace;
O refresh us, O refresh us, Travelling thro' this wilderness.

May the fruits of thy salvation In our hearts and lives abound;
May thy presence, may thy presence With us evermore be found.

THE INVITATION.

1.
Come, ye sinners, poor and needy,
  Weak and wounded, sick and sore ;
Jesus ready stands to save you,
  Full of pity, love and power ;
    He is able,
He is willing : doubt no more.

2.
Come, ye weary, heavy-laden,
  Bruised and mangled by the fall ;
If you tarry till you're better,
  You will never come at all ;
    Not the righteous—
Sinners, Jesus came to call.

3.
Let not conscience make you linger,
  Nor of fitness fondly dream ;
All the fitness he requireth
  Is to feel your need of him :
    This he gives you,—
'Tis the Spirit's glimm'ring beam.

CHILDREN EXHORTED.

1.
Children, hear the melting story
  Of the Lamb that once was slain ;
'Tis the Lord of life and glory :
  Shall he plead with you in vain ?
    O, receive him,
And salvation now obtain.

2.
Yield no more to sin and folly,
  So displeasing in his sight :
Jesus loves the pure and holy ;
  They alone are his delight ;
    Seek his favor,
And your hearts to him unite.

3.
All your sins to him confessing
  Who is ready to forgive,
Seek the Saviour's richest blessing ;
  On his precious name believe :
    He is waiting :
Will you not his grace receive ?

GOD IS LOVE. 8s & 7s.

D. H. NORRIS.

Lively.

1. God is love; his mercy brightens All the paths in which we rove;
2. Chance and change are busy ev-er; Man decays, and a-ges move;
3. E'en the hour that darkest seemeth Will his changeless goodness prove;
4. He with earth-ly cares en twin-eth Hope and com-fort from a-bove;

Bliss he wakes, and woe he lightens, God is wisdom. God is love.
But his mer-cy waneth nev-er; God is wisdom, God is love.
From the gloom his brightness streameth; God is wisdom. God is love.
Ev-'ry-where his glo-ry shin-eth; God is wisdom. God is love.

PRAISE TO CHRIST THE AUTHOR OF SALVATION.

Crown his head with endless blessing,
  Who, in God. the Father's name,
With compassion never ceasing,
  Comes, salvation to proclaim.

2

Lo. Jehovah, we adore thee,—
  Thee, our Saviour,—thee, our God;
From thy throne let beams of glory
  Shine through all the world abroad,

3

Jesus, thee our Saviour hailing,
  Thee our God in praise we own;
Highest honors, never failing,
  Rise eternal round thy throne.

4

Now, ye saints, his power confessing,
  In your grateful strains adore;
For his mercy, never ceasing,
  Flows, and flows forevermore.

PRAISE THE LORD.

Praise the Lord; ye heavens, adore him;
  Praise him angels, in the height;
Sun and moon, rejoice before him;
  Praise him, all ye stars of light.

2

Praise the Lord, for he hath spoken;
  Worlds his mighty voice obeyed;
Laws, which never can be broken,
  For their guidance he hath made.

3

Praise the Lord, for he is glorious;
  Never shall his promise fail;
God hath made his saints victorious;
  Sin and death shall not prevail.

4

Praise the God of our salvation;
  Hosts on high, his power proclaim;
Heaven and earth, and all creation,
  Praise and magnify his name.

HOLY FATHER. 8s, 7s & 4.

1864.

Slow, and with expression.

1. Ho-ly Father, we adore thee, As dis-ci-ples of thy Son;
2. May the words by Je-sus spoken, From our sins to set us free,

And whene'er we come before thee, Be our hearts and voi-ces one;
May the bread by Je-sus bro-ken, Near the lake of Gal-i-lee,

TRIO.

Ev-er praying, ev-er praying, "Let thy ho-ly will be done."
Ho-ly Father, Ho-ly Father, Feed our souls and guide to thee.

THE PILGRIM'S GUIDE AND GUARDIAN.

1
Guide me, O thou great Jehovah,
 Pilgrim through this barren land :
I am weak—but thou art mighty ;
 Hold me with thy powerful hand ;
  Bread of heaven,
 Feed me till I want no more.

2
Open now the crystal fountain,
 Whence the healing waters flow ;
Let the fiery, cloudy pillar,
 Lead me all my journey through :
  Strong Deliv'rer,
 Be thou still my strength and shield.

3
When I tread the verge of Jordan,
 Bid my anxious fears subside :
Bear me through the swelling current,
 Land me safe on Canaan's side ;
  Songs of praises
 I will ever give to thee.

GREENVILLE. 8s, 7s & 4s.

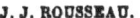

J. J. ROUSSEAU.

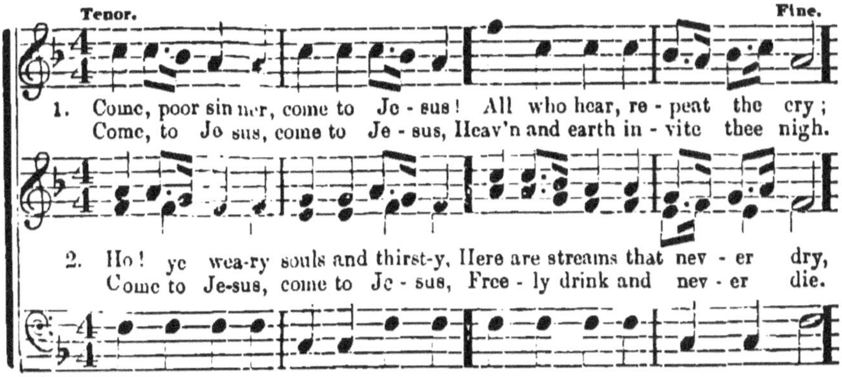
Tenor.
Fine.
1. Come, poor sin ner, come to Je - sus! All who hear, re - peat the cry;
Come, to Je sus, come to Je - sus, Heav'n and earth in - vite thee nigh.
2. Ho! ye wea-ry souls and thirst-y, Here are streams that nev - er dry,
Come to Je-sus, come to Je - sus, Free - ly drink and nev - er die.

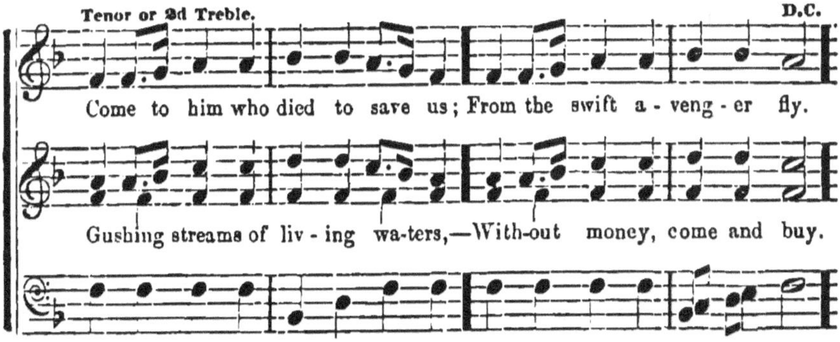
Tenor or 2d Treble.
D.C.
Come to him who died to save us; From the swift a - veng - er fly.
Gushing streams of liv - ing wa-ters,—With-out money, come and buy.

CHILDREN EXHORTED.

Children, hear the melting story
Of the Lamb that once was slain:
'Tis the Lord of life and glory:
Shall he plead with you in vain?
O, receive him,
And salvation now obtain.

2

Yield no more to sin and folly,
So displeasing in his sight:
Jesus loves the pure and holy;
They alone are his delight;
Seek his favor,
And your hearts to him unite.

3

All your sins to him confessing,
Who is ready to forgive,
Seek the Saviour's richest blessing;
On his precious name believe;
He is waiting;
Will you not his grace receive?

THE EXPIRING SAVIOUR.

Hark! the voice of love and mercy
Sounds aloud from Calvary:
See! it rends the rocks asunder,
Shakes the earth, and veils the sky:
"It is finished!"
Hear the dying Saviour cry.

2

"It is finished!"—O, what pleasure
Do these charming words afford!
Heavenly blessings, without measure,
Flow to us through Christ the Lord:
"It is finished!"
Saints, the dying words record.

DOXOLOGY.

Great Jehovah, we adore thee,
God the Father, God the Son,
God the Spirit, joined in glory
On the same eternal throne:
Endless praises
To Jehovah, three in one.

"GENTLY LORD." 8s & 7s.

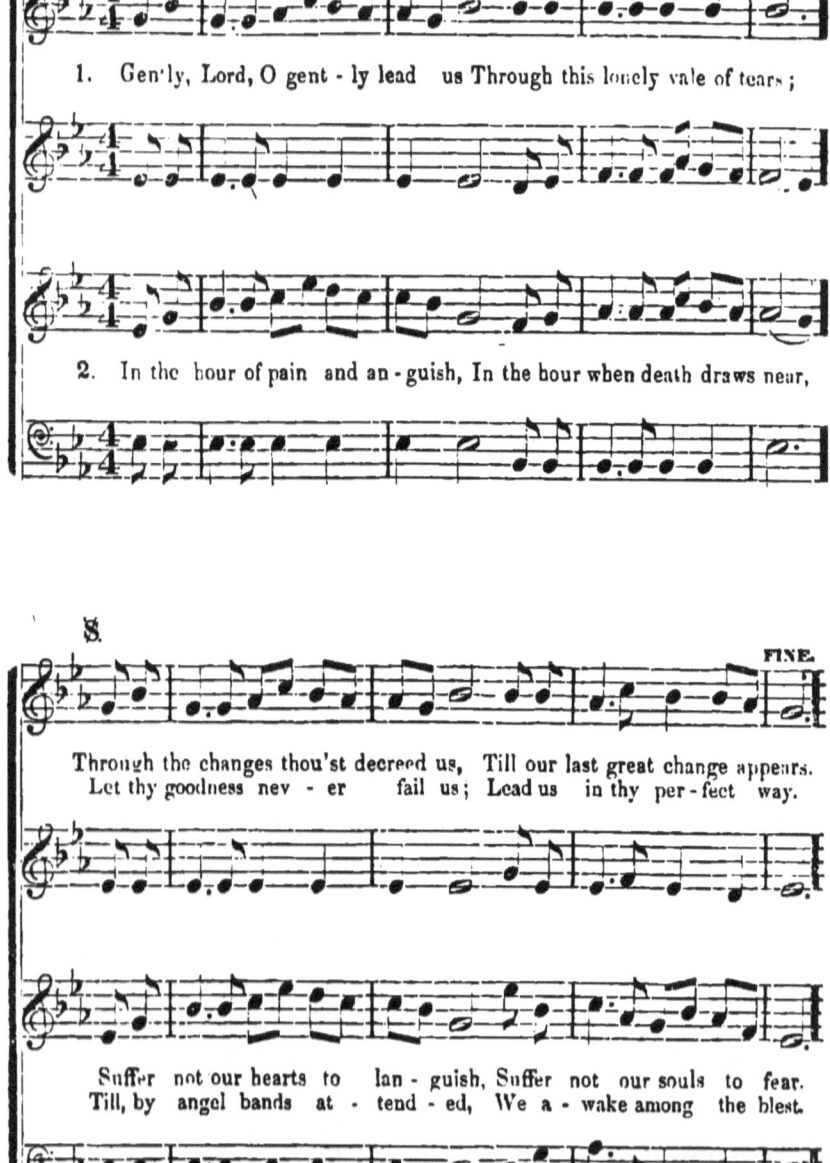

1. Gently, Lord, O gent-ly lead us Through this lonely vale of tears;
2. In the hour of pain and an-guish, In the hour when death draws near,

Through the changes thou'st decreed us, Till our last great change appears.
Let thy goodness nev - er fail us; Lead us in thy per-fect way.

Suffer not our hearts to lan - guish, Suffer not our souls to fear.
Till, by angel bands at - tend - ed, We a - wake among the blest.

"GENTLY LORD." Concluded.

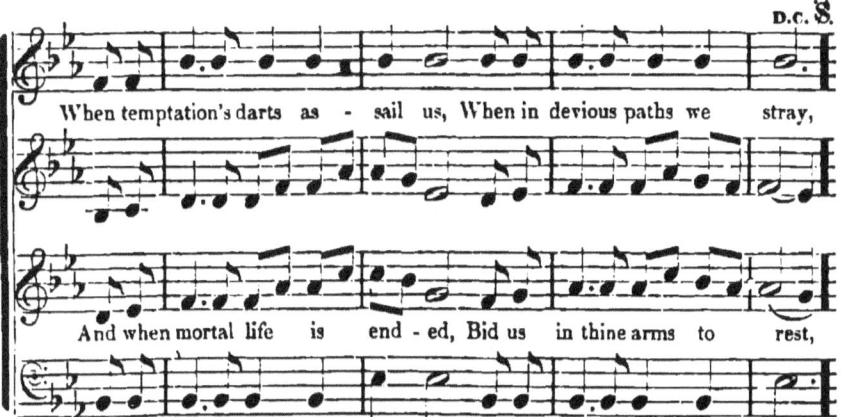

When temptation's darts as-sail us, When in devious paths we stray,
And when mortal life is end-ed, Bid us in thine arms to rest,

14. BLESSEDNESS OF THE RIGHTEOUS.

1 Cease, ye mourners, cease to languish,
O'er the grave of those you love ;
Pain and death,and night and anguish,
Enter not the world above.

2 While our silent steps are straying,
Lonely thro' night's deepening shade,
Glory's brightest beams are playing
Round the immortal spirit's head.

3 Light and peace at once deriving
From the hand of God most high,
In his glorious presence living
They shall never—never die.

4 Endless pleasure, pain excluding,
Sickness there no more can come ;
There, no fear of wo intruding.
Sheds o'er heaven a moment's gloom.

15. CONFIDENCE IN GOD.

1 Saviour, breathe an evening blessing,
E'er repose our spirits seal ;
Sin and want we come confessing ;
Thou canst save and thou canst heal.

2 Though destruction walk around us,
Though the arrows past us fly,
Angel guards from thee surrounds us ;
We are safe, if thou art nigh.

3 Though the night be dark and dreary,
Darkness cannot hide from thee ;
Thou art He who, never weary,
Watchest where thy people be.

4 Should swift death this night o'ertake us,
And command us to the tomb,
May the morn in heaven awake us,
Clad in bright, eternal bloom.

16 HITHERTO HATH THE LORD HELPED US.

Come, thou fount of every blessing,
Tune my heart to sing thy grace :
Streams of mercy, never ceasing,
Call for songs of loudest praise.
Teach me some melodious sonnet,
Sung by flaming tongues above ;
Praise the mount—I'm fixed upon it ;
Mount of thy redeeming love !

2 Here I'll raise mine Ebenezer ;
Hither by thy help I'm come ;
And I hope, by thy good pleasure,
Safely to arrive at home.
Jesus sought me when a stranger,
Wand'ring from the fold of God,
He, to rescue me from danger,
Interposed his precious blood.

3 O ! to grace how great a debtor
Daily I'm constrain'd to be !
Let thy goodness, like a fetter,
Bind my wand'ring heart to thee :
Prone to wander, Lord, I feel it—
Prone to leave the God I love ;
Here's my heart, O take and seal it ;
Seal it for thy courts above.

"FOREVER WITH THE LORD." Concluded.

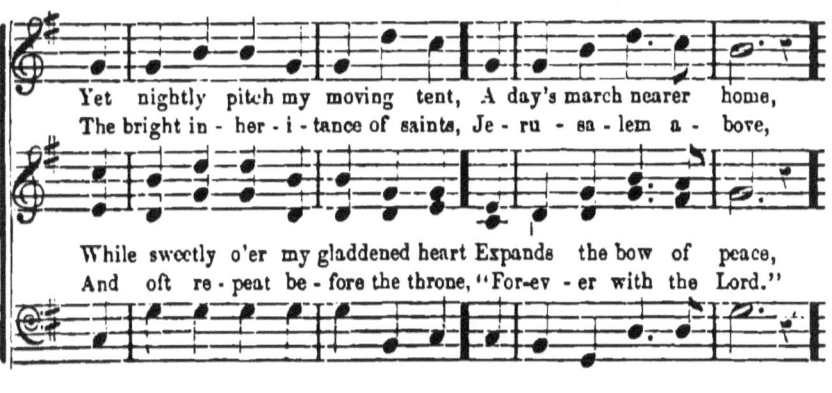

Yet nightly pitch my moving tent, A day's march nearer home,
The bright in-her-i-tance of saints, Je-ru-sa-lem a-bove,

While sweetly o'er my gladdened heart Expands the bow of peace,
And oft re-peat be-fore the throne, "For-ev-er with the Lord."

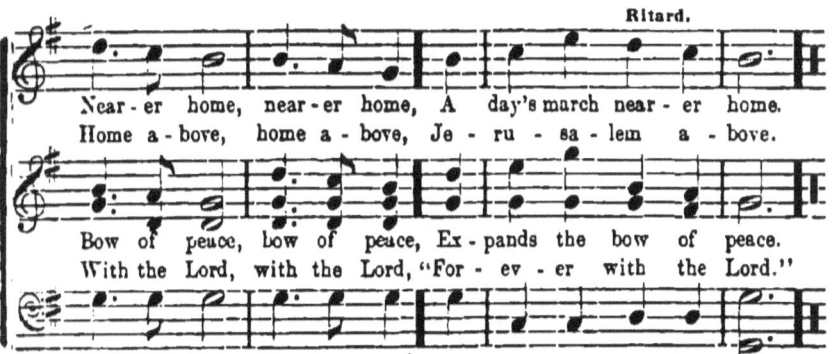

Ritard.

Near-er home, near-er home, A day's march near-er home.
Home a-bove, home a-bove, Je-ru-sa-lem a-bove.

Bow of peace, bow of peace, Ex-pands the bow of peace.
With the Lord, with the Lord, "For-ev-er with the Lord."

DELIGHT IN GOD.

Lord! I delight in thee,
  And on thy care depend;
To thee in every trouble flee,
  My best, my only friend.
When nature's streams are dried,
  Thy fulness is the same;
With this will I be satisfied,
  And glory in thy name.
In thy name, in thy name,
  And glory in thy name.

2

Who made my heaven secure,
  Will here all good provide:
While Christ is rich, can I be poor?
  What can I want beside?
I cast my care on thee,
  I triumph and adore:
Henceforth my great concerns shall be
  To love and please thee more,
Please thee more, please thee more,
  To love and please thee more.

FOR PERFECT SUBMISSION.

I want a heart to pray,—
  To pray, and never cease;
Never to murmur at thy stay,
  Or wish my suff'rings less.
This blessing, above all,—
  Always to pray,—I want;
Out of the deep on thee to call,
  And never, never faint;
Never faint, never faint,
  And never, never faint.

2

I rest upon thy word,—
  The promise is for me;
My succor and salvation, Lord,
  Shall surely come from thee:
But let me still abide,
  Nor from my hope remove,
'Till thou my patient spirit guide
  Into thy perfect love.
Perfect love, perfect love,
  Into thy perfect love.

MORNING HYMN. S. M.

With Expression.

1. Se-rene I laid me down, Beneath his guar-dian care: I slept—and I a-woke, and found My kind pre-serv-er near.
2. Thus does thine arm sup-port This weak, de-fence-less frame; This fee-ble spir-it pants be-neath, The pleas-ing, pain-ful load.
3. O, how shall I re-pay The bounties of my God? But whence these favors, Lord, to me, All worthless as I am?
4. My life I would re-new De-vote, O Lord, to thee; And in thy ser-vice I would spend A long e-ter-ni-ty.

CHRIST OUR LORD.

My Saviour, fill my soul
 With holiness and peace;
Arise with healing in thy wings;
 Bid sin and doubting cease.

2
May things beneath the sky
 Engross my heart no more;
Be thou my first, my chief delight,
 My soul's unbounded store.

3
In thee all treasures lie;
 From thee all blessings flow;
Thou art the bliss of saints above,
 The joy of saints below.

4
O, come and make me thine,
 A sinner saved by grace:
Then shall I sing, with loudest strains,
 In heaven, thy dwelling-place.

PRAYER FOR DELIVERANCE.

Like Israel, Lord, am I;
 My soul is at a stand;
A sea before, a host behind,
 And rocks on either hand.

2
O Lord, I cry to thee,
 And would thy word obey;
Bid me advance; and, through the sea,
 Create a new-made way.

3
The time of greatest straits
 Thy chosen time has been
To manifest thy power is great,
 And make thy glory seen.

4
O, send deliverance down;
 Display the arm divine;
So shall the praise be all thy own,
 And I be doubly thine.

SALVATION'S FREE. S. M.

Arr. for this work.

1. O! for a shout of joy To God, our heavenly King!
CHO.—I'm glad sal-va-tion's free, I'm glad sal-va-tion's free,

2. Je-sus, as-cends on high; His heaven-ly guards a-round
3. While an-gels praise their King, Let mor-tals learn their strains;

Let eve-ry land their tongues employ, And hymns of triumph sing.
Sal-va-tion's free for you and me, I'm glad sal-va-tion's free.

At-tend him ris-ing through the sky, With trumpet's joy-ful sound.
Let all the earth his honors sing; O'er all the earth he reigns.

GLORY BEGUN BELOW.

Come, ye that love the Lord,
 And let your joys be known ;
Join in a song with sweet accord,
 While ye surround his throne.
CHO.—I'm glad salvation's free,
 I'm glad salvation's free,
 Salvation's free for you and me,
 I'm glad salvation's free.

2
Let those refuse to sing
 Who never knew our God,
But servants of the heavenly King
 May speak their joys abroad.

3
There we shall see his face,
 And never, never sin ;
There, from the rivers of his grace,
 Drink endless pleasures in :

4
Yea, and before we rise
 To that immortal state,
The thoughts of such amazing bliss
 Should constant joys create.

THE GOODLY LAND.

Far from these scenes of night,
 Unbounded glories rise,
And realms of joy and pure delight,
 Unknown to mortal eyes.
CHO.—There'll be no parting there,
 There'll be no parting there,
 In heaven alone, no parting's known,
 There'll be no parting there.

2
Fair land!—could mortal eyes
 But half its charms explore,
How would our spirits long to rise,
 And dwell on earth no more !

3
No cloud those regions know.—
 Realms ever bright and fair ;
For sin, the source of mortal woe,
 Can never enter there.

4
O may the prospect fire
 Our hearts with ardent love,
Till wings of faith, and strong desire,
 Bear every thought above.

BOYLSTON. S. M.
L. MASON. *By permission.*

1. A charge to keep I have, A God to glo-ri-fy;
   A nev-er dy-ing soul to save, And fit it for the sky.
2. To serve the pres-ent age, My call-ing to ful-fil,—
   O, may it all my powers en-gage, To do my master's will.
3. Arm me with jeal-ous care, As in thy sight to live;
   And O, thy servant, Lord, prepare, A strict account to give.
4. Help me to watch and pray, And on thy-self re-ly,
   As-sured, if I my trust be-tray, I shall for-ev-er die.

KINDNESS TO OUR FRAILTY.

The pity of the Lord,
  To those that fear his name,
Is such as tender parents feel;
  He knows our feeble frame.

2

He knows we are but dust,
  Scattered with every breath;
His anger, like a rising wind,
  Can send us swift to death.

3

Our days are as the grass,
  Or like the morning flower;
When blasting winds sweep o'er the field,
  It withers in an hour.

4

But thy compassions, Lord,
  To endless years endure;
And children's children ever find
  Thy words of promise sure.

THE ALL-SUFFICIENT PORTION.

And can I yet delay
  My little all to give?
To tear my soul from earth away
  For Jesus to receive?

2

Nay, but I yield, I yield;
  I can hold out no more;
I sink, by dying love compell'd,
  And own thee conqueror.

3

Though late, I all forsake;
  My friends, my all, resign:
Gracious Redeemer, take, O take,
  And seal me ever thine.

4

Come, and possess me whole
  Nor hence again remove;
Settle and fix my wav'ring soul
  With all thy weight of love.

ST. THOMAS. S. M.   A. WILLIAMS.   85

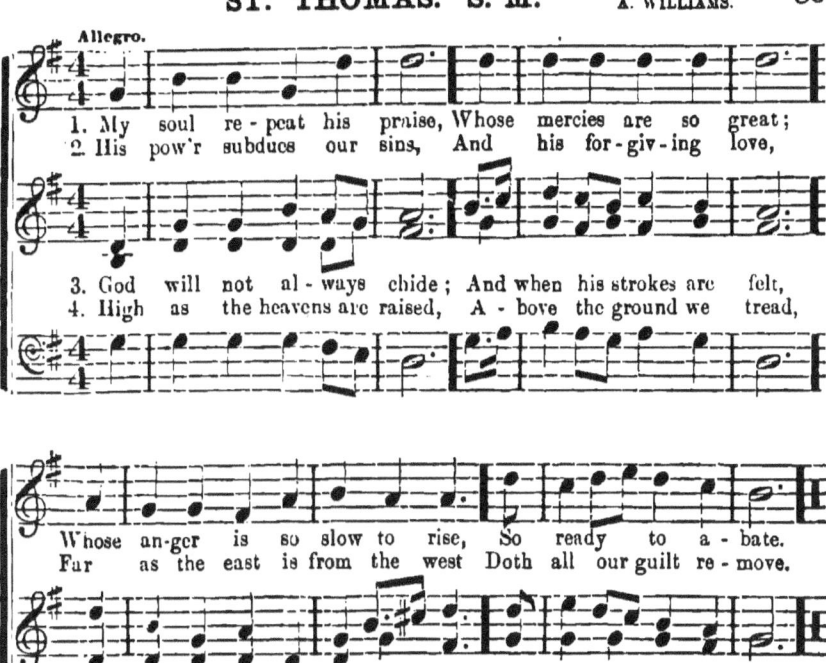

1. My soul re-peat his praise, Whose mercies are so great;
2. His pow'r subdues our sins, And his for-giv-ing love,
3. God will not al-ways chide; And when his strokes are felt,
4. High as the heavens are raised, A-bove the ground we tread,

Whose an-ger is so slow to rise, So ready to a-bate.
Far as the east is from the west Doth all our guilt re-move.
His strokes are few-er than our crimes, And light-er than our guilt.
So far the rich-es of his grace, Our high-est thoughts exceed.

INVITATION TO THE HOUSE OF GOD.

Come to the house of prayer,
  O thou afflicted, come;
The God of peace shall meet thee there;
  He makes that house his home.

2

Come to the house of praise,
  Ye who are happy now;
In sweet accord your voices raise,
  In kindred homage bow.

3

Ye aged, hither come,
  For ye have felt his love;
Soon shall your trembling tongues be dumb,
  Your lips forget to move.

4

Ye young, before his throne,
  Come, bow; your voices raise;
Let not your hearts his praise disown,
  Who gives the power to praise.

DELIGHT IN ORDINANCES.

Welcome, sweet day of rest,
  That saw the Lord arise:
Welcome to this reviving breast,
  And these rejoicing eyes!

2

The King himself comes near,
  And feasts his saints to-day;
Here we may sit, and see him here,
  And love, and praise, and pray.

3

One day in such a place,
  Where thou, my God, art seen,
Is sweeter than ten thousand days
  Of pleasurable sin.

4

My willing soul would stay
  In such a frame as this,
And sit and sing herself away
  To everlasting bliss.

86   CORONATION. C. M.   O. HOLDEN.

3
Let every kindred, every tribe
On this terrestrial ball,
To him all majesty ascribe,
And crown him Lord of all.

4
O that with yonder sacred throng
We at his feet may fall;
We'll join the everlasting song,
And crown him Lord of all.

WARWICK. C. M. — STANLEY.

1. Lord, in the morning thou shalt hear My voice as-cend-ing high:
2. Up to the hills where Christ is gone, To plead for all his saints;
3. Thou art a God be-fore whose sight The wick-ed shall not stand;
4. O may thy Spirit guide my feet In ways of righteous-ness;

To thee will I di-rect my prayer,—To thee lift up mine eye:—
Pre-sent-ing, at the Fa-ther's throne, Our songs and our complaints.
Sin-ners shall ne'er be thy de-light, Nor dwell at thy right hand.
Make ev-'ry path of du-ty straight, And plain be-fore my face.

FOUNDED ON A ROCK.

With stately towers and bulwarks strong,
Unrivall'd and alone,—
Loved theme of many a sacred song,—
God's holy city shone.

2
Thus fair was Zion's chosen seat,
The glory of all lands;
Yet fairer, and in strength complete,
The Christian temple stands.

3
The faithful of each clime and age
This glorious Church compose;
Built on a Rock, with idle rage
The threat'ning tempest blows.

4
Fear not; though hostile bands alarm,
Thy God is thy defence;
And weak and powerless every arm
Against Omnipotence.

INVOKING GOD'S PRESENCE AND BLESSING.

Within thy house, O Lord our God,
In majesty appear;
Make this a place of thine abode,
And shed thy blessings here.

2
As we thy mercy-seat surround,
Thy Spirit, Lord, impart:
And let thy Gospel's joyful sound,
With power reach every heart.

3
Here let the blind their sight obtain;
Here give the mourner rest;
Let Jesus here triumphant reign,
Enthroned in every breast.

4
Here let the voice of sacred joy
And fervent prayer arise,
Till higher strains our tongues employ,
In bliss beyond the skies.

THE BIBLE. Concluded.

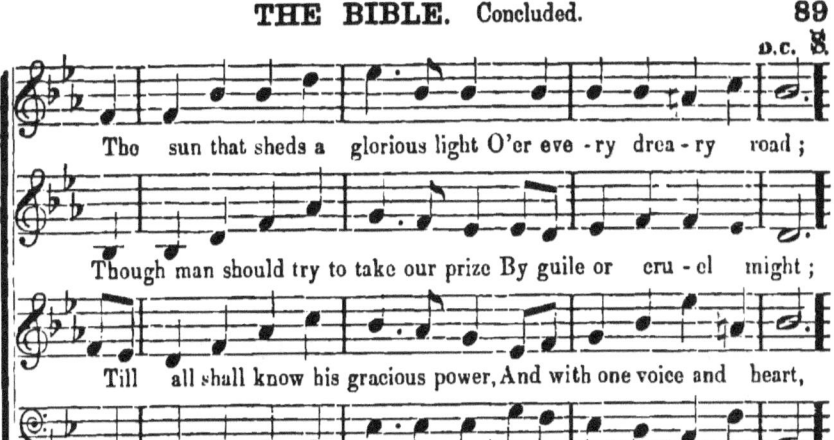

The sun that sheds a glorious light O'er eve-ry drea-ry road;
Though man should try to take our prize By guile or cru-el might;
Till all shall know his gracious power, And with one voice and heart,

3. THE HEAVENLY CANAAN. C. M.

1 There is a land of pure delight,
  Where saints immortal reign;
  Infinite day excludes the night,
  And pleasures banish pain.

2 There everlasting spring abides,
  And never with'ring flowers:
  Death, like a narrow sea, divides
  This heavenly land from ours.

3 Sweet fields beyond the swelling flood
  Stand dress'd in living green;
  So to the Jews old Canaan stood,
  While Jordan rolled between.

4 Could we but climb where Moses stood,
  And view the landscape o'er,
  Not Jordan's stream, nor death's cold flood,
  Should fright us from the shore.

4. THE PROMISED LAND. C. M.

1 On Jordan's stormy banks I stand,
  And cast a wishful eye
  To Canaan's fair and happy land,
  Where my possessions lie.

2 O the transporting, rapturous scene,
  That rises to my sight!
  Sweet fields array'd in living green,
  And rivers of delight.

3 There generous fruits that never fail,
  On trees immortal grow;
  There rock, and hill, and brook, and vale,
  With milk and honey flow.

4 O'er all those wide extended plains
  Shines one eternal day;
  There God the Son forever reigns,
  And scatters night away.

5 No chilling winds, or pois'nous breath,
  Can reach that healthful shore;
  Sickness and sorrow, pain and death,
  Are felt and fear'd no more.

6 Filled with delight my raptured soul
  Would here no longer stay:
  Though Jordan's waves around me roll,
  Fearless I'd launch away.

5.
A PERFECT HEART THE REDEEMER'S THRONE.

1 O for a heart to praise my God,
  A heart from sin set free;
  A heart that always feels thy blood,
  So freely spilt for me;—

2 A heart resigned, submissive, meek,
  My great Redeemer's throne;
  Where only Christ is heard to speak,
  Where Jesus reigns alone.

3 O for a lowly, contrite heart,
  Believing, true, and clean;
  Which neither life, nor death can part
  From Him that dwells within:—

4 A heart in every thought renew'd,
  And full of love divine;
  Perfect, and right, and pure, and good,
  A copy, Lord of thine.

WARD. L. M.

Scotch.

1. How blest the righteous when he dies! When sinks a wea-ry soul to rest;
2. So fades a summer cloud a-way; So sinks the gale when storms are o'er;
3. A ho-ly qui-et reigns around, A calm which life nor death de-stroys;
4. Life's la-bor done, as sinks the clay, Light from its load the spir-it flies,

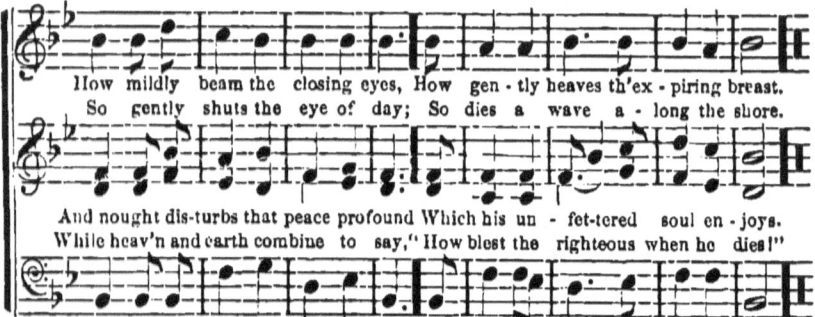

How mildly beam the closing eyes, How gen-tly heaves th'ex-piring breast.
So gently shuts the eye of day; So dies a wave a-long the shore.
And nought dis-turbs that peace profound Which his un-fet-tered soul en-joys.
While heav'n and earth combine to say, "How blest the righteous when he dies!"

SINNERS INVITED TO IMMEDIATE REPENTANCE.

1.
While life prolongs its precious light,
　Mercy is found, and peace is given;
But soon, ah, soon, approaching night
　Shall blot out every hope of heaven.

2.
While God invites, how blest the day!
　How sweet the gospel's charming sound!
Come, sinners, haste, O, haste away,
　While yet a pard'ning God is found.

3.
Soon, borne on time's most rapid wing,
　Shall death command you to the grave,
Before his bar your spirits bring,
　And none be found to hear or save.

4.
In that lone land of deep despair,
　No Sabbath's heavenly light shall rise,
No God regard your bitter prayer,
　No Saviour call you to the skies.

EXHORTATION TO PRAYER.

1.
What various hind'rances we meet,
　In coming to a mercy seat!
Yet who that knows the worth of prayer,
　But wishes to be often there?

2.
Prayer makes the darkened cloud withdraw;
　Prayer climbs the ladder Jacob saw;
Gives exercise to faith and love,
　Brings every blessing from above.

3.
Restraining prayer, we cease to fight;
Prayer makes the Christian's armour bright;
And Satan trembles when he sees
　The weakest saint upon his knees.

4.
While Moses stood with arms spread wide,
　Success was found on Israel's side;
But when through weariness they failed,
　That moment Amalek prevailed.

2.
I tremble, lest the wrath divine
  Which bruises now my wretched soul,
Should bruise this wretched soul of mine,
  Long as eternal ages roll.

3.
I deprecate that death alone,
  That endless banishment from thee;
O, save, and give me to thy Son,
  Who trembled, wept, and bled for me.

NEWTON. L. M.

THE GOSPEL FEAST.

1.
Come, sinners, to the gospel feast;
Let every soul be Jesus' guest:
Ye need not one be left behind,
For God hath bidden all mankind.

2.
Sent by my Lord, on you I call;
The invitation is to all:—
Come all the world! come, sinner, thou,
All things in Christ are ready now.

3.
Come, all ye souls by sin oppress'd,
Ye restless wand'rers after rest;
Ye poor, and maim'd, and halt, and blind,
In Christ a hearty welcome find.

4.
My message as from God receive;
Ye all may come to Christ and live:
O let his love your hearts constrain,
Nor suffer him to die in vain.

OLD HUNDRED. L. M.

Unknown.

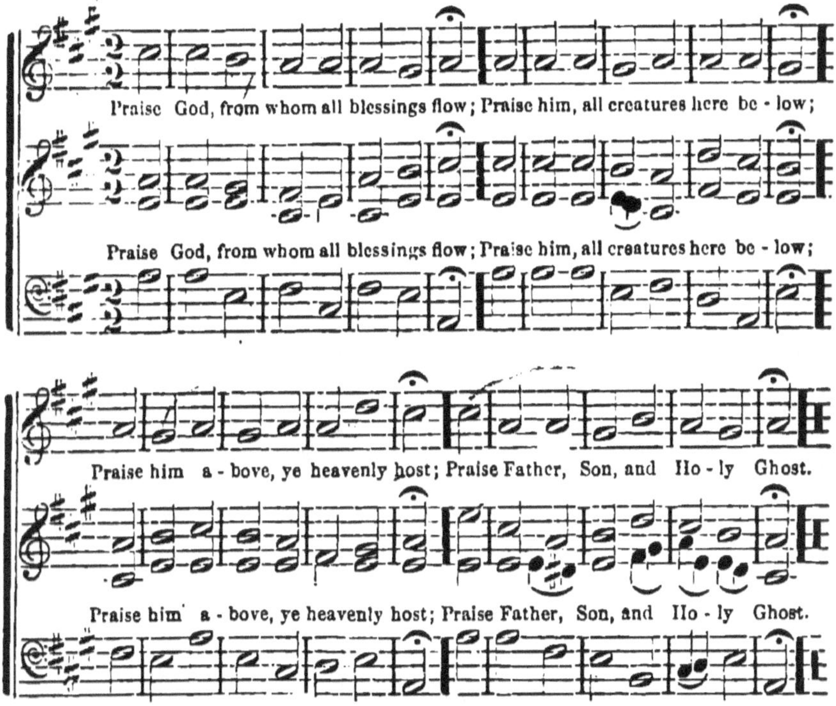
Praise God, from whom all blessings flow; Praise him, all creatures here be - low;
Praise God, from whom all blessings flow; Praise him, all creatures here be - low;
Praise him a - bove, ye heavenly host; Praise Father, Son, and Ho - ly Ghost.
Praise him a - bove, ye heavenly host; Praise Father, Son, and Ho - ly Ghost.

MY HEAVENLY HOME.*

From "W. S. Harp."

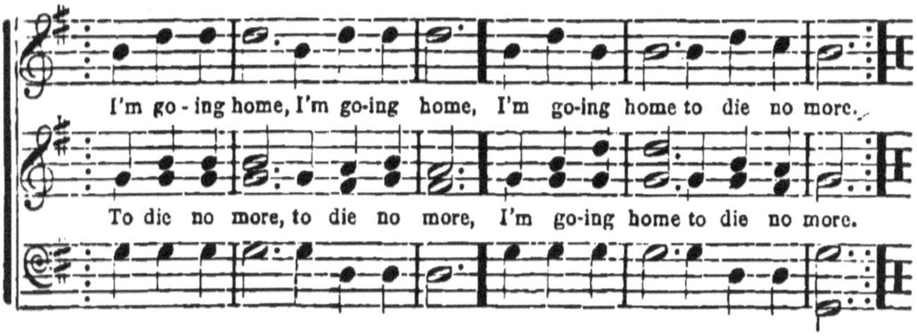
I'm go - ing home, I'm go-ing home, I'm go-ing home to die no more.
To die no more, to die no more, I'm go-ing home to die no more.

THE CHRISTIAN'S PROSPECT.

What sinners value I resign;
Lord, 'tis enough that thou art mine;
I shall behold thy blissful face,
And stand complete in righteousness.
I'm going home, &c.

2.

This life's a dream—an empty show;
But that bright world to which I go
Hath joys substantial and sincere:
When shall I wake and find me there?
I'm going home, &c.

* This tune may be used as chorus to Newton, or sung by itself.

ZEPHYR. L. M.

W. B. BRADBURY.
From "The Jubilee." By permission.

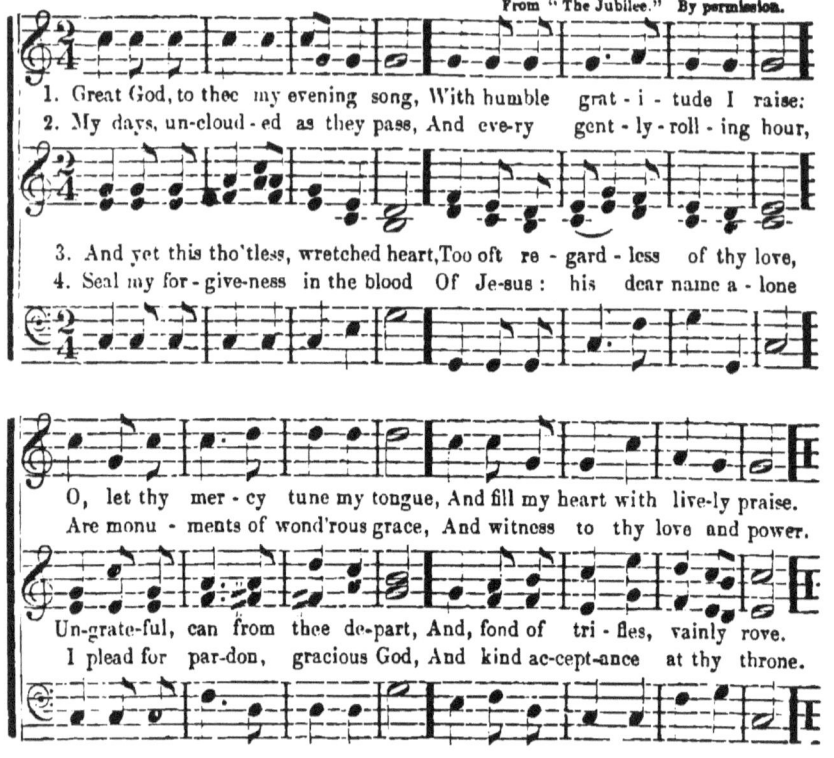

1. Great God, to thee my evening song, With humble gratitude I raise:
O, let thy mercy tune my tongue, And fill my heart with lively praise.

2. My days, unclouded as they pass, And every gently-rolling hour,
Are monuments of wond'rous grace, And witness to thy love and power.

3. And yet this tho'tless, wretched heart, Too oft regardless of thy love,
Ungrateful, can from thee depart, And, fond of trifles, vainly rove.

4. Seal my forgiveness in the blood Of Jesus: his dear name alone
I plead for pardon, gracious God, And kind acceptance at thy throne.

Communion.

CONSECRATION IN VIEW OF THE CROSS.

When I survey the wondrous cross,
On which the Prince of glory died,
My richest gain I count but loss,
And pour contempt on all my pride.

2.
Forbid it, Lord, that I should boast,
Save in the death of Christ, my God;
All the vain things that charm me most,
I sacrifice them to his blood.

3.
See, from his head, his hands, his feet,
Sorrow and love flow mingled down:
Did e'er such love and sorrow meet,
Or thorns compose so rich a crown.

4.
Were all the realm of nature mine,
That were a present far too small;
Love so amazing, so divine,
Demands my soul, my life, my all.

Funerals.

THE CHRISTIAN'S PARTING HOUR.

How sweet the hour of closing day,
When all is peaceful and serene,
And when the sun, with cloudless ray,
Sheds mellow lustre o'er the scene!

2.
Such is the Christian's parting hour,
So peacefully he sinks to rest;
When faith, endued from heaven with pow'r
Sustains and cheers his languid breast.

3.
A beam from heaven is sent to cheer
The pilgrim on his gloomy road;
And angels are attending near,
To bear him to their bright abode.

4.
Who would not wish to die like those
Whom God's own Spirit deigns to bless?
To sink into that soft repose,
Then wake to perfect happiness?

THE GOOD SHEPHERD. L. M. 6 lines. ✻ 95

MADISON. 8s.

S. B. POND

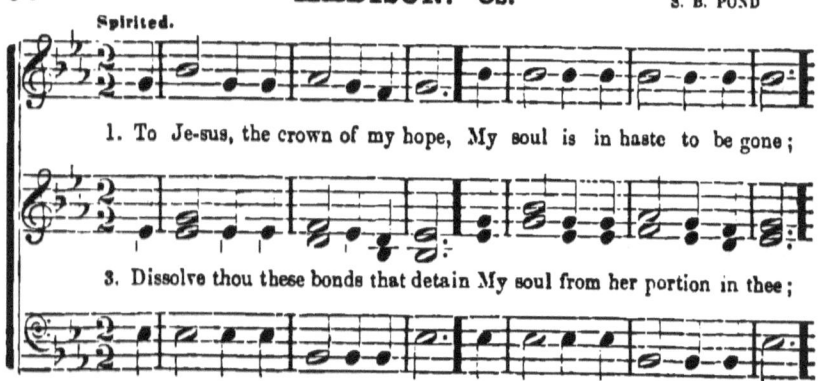

1. To Jesus, the crown of my hope, My soul is in haste to be gone;
3. Dissolve thou these bonds that detain My soul from her portion in thee;

O, bear me, ye cher-u-bim, up, And waft me a-way to his throne.
O, strike off this ad-a-mant chain, And make me e-ter-nal-ly free.

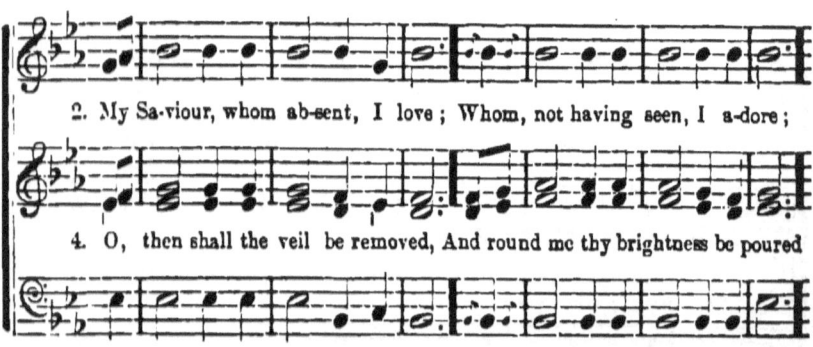

2. My Saviour, whom ab-sent, I love; Whom, not having seen, I a-dore;
4. O, then shall the veil be removed, And round me thy brightness be poured

MADISON. Concluded.

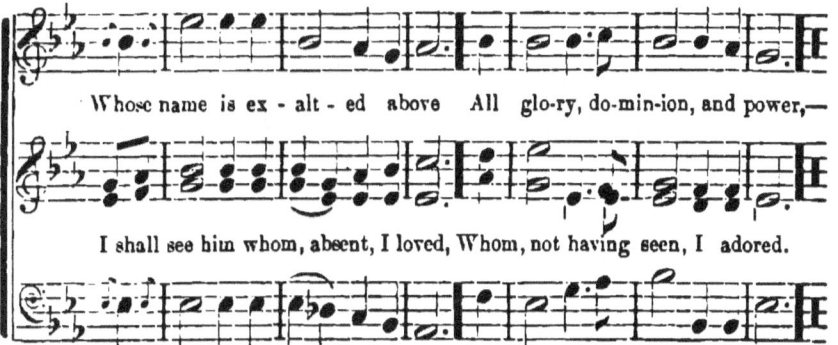

Whose name is ex-alt-ed above All glo-ry, do-min-ion, and power,—
I shall see him whom, absent, I loved, Whom, not having seen, I adored.

CHRISTIAN UNION.

From whence doth this union arise,
  That hatred is conquered by love?
That fastens our souls in such ties
  As nature and time can't remove?
It cannot in Eden be found,
  Nor yet in a paradise lost;
It grows on Immanuel's ground,
  And Jesus' rich blood it did cost.

2
My friends are so dear unto me,
  Our hearts are united in love:
Where Jesus is gone we shall be,
  In yonder blest mansions above.
Then why so unwilling to part,
  Since there we shall all meet again?
Engraved on Immanuel's heart,
  At distance we cannot remain.

3
O, when shall we see that bright day,
  And join with the angels above,
Set free from these prisons of clay,
  United with Jesus in love!
With Jesus we ever shall reign,
  And all his bright glories shall see,
And sing, Hallelujah! amen!
  Amen! even so let it be.

FOLLOWING THE LAMB.

What now is my object and aim?
  What now is my hope and desire?
To follow the heavenly Lamb,
  And after his image aspire:
My hope is all centred in thee;
  I trust to recover thy love;
On earth thy salvation to see,
  And then to enjoy it above.

HAPPINESS OF HEAVEN.

We speak of the realms of the bless'd,
  That country so bright and so fair;
And oft are its glories confess'd,
  But what must it be to be there?
We speak of its pathway of gold,
  Of its walls decked with jewels most rare,
Of its wonders and pleasures untold;
  But what must it be to be there?

2
We speak of its freedom from sin,
  From sorrow, temptation, and care—
From trials without and within;
  But what must it be to be there?
Then let us 'midst pleasure or woe,
  For heaven our spirits prepare;
And shortly we also shall know,
  And feel what it is to be there.

SELF-CONSECRATION.

O Jesus, delight of my soul,
  My Saviour, my Shepherd divine,
I yield to thy blessed control;
  My body and spirit are thine:
Thy love I can never deserve,
  That bids me be happy in thee;
My God and my King I will serve,
  Whose favour is heaven to me.

2
How can I thy goodness repay,
  By nature so weak and defiled?
Myself I have given away;
  O call me thine own blessed child:
And art thou my Father above?
  Will Jesus abide in my heart?
O bind me so fast with thy love,
  That I never from thee shall depart.

"ARISE, MY SOUL, ARISE." H. M.

ARISE, MY SOUL. Concluded.

on his bands, My name is writ - - ten on his hands.

throne of grace, And sprinkles now the throne of grace.

sin - ner die, Nor let that ran - som'd sin - - ner die.

4
The Father hears him pray,
  His dear anointed One :
He cannot turn away
  The presence of his Son :
His Spirit answers to the blood,
And tells me I am born of God.

5
My God is reconciled ;
  His pard'ning voice I hear :
He owns me for his child;
  I can no longer fear :
With confidence I now draw nigh,
And Father, Abba, Father, cry.

7. THE JUBILEE TRUMPET. H. M.

1
Blow ye the trumpet, blow
  The gladly-solemn sound ;
Let all the nations know,
  To earth's remotest bound,
The year of jubilee is come ;
Return, ye ransom'd sinners, home.

2
Jesus, our great High Priest,
  Hath full atonement made :
Ye weary spirits, rest ;
  Ye mournful souls, be glad :
The year of jubilee is come;
Return, ye ransom'd sinners, home.

3
Extol the Lamb of God,—
  The all-atoning Lamb ;
Redemption in his blood
  Throughout the world proclaim :
The year of jubilee is come ;
Return, ye ransom'd sinners, home.

4
Ye slaves of sin and hell,
  Your liberty receive,
And safe in Jesus dwell,
  And blest in Jesus live :
The year of jubilee is come ;
Return, ye ransom'd sinners, home.

5
Ye who have sold for naught
  Your heritage above,
Shall have it back unbought,
  The gift of Jesus' love :
The year of jubilee is come ;
Return, ye ransom'd sinners, home.

6
The gospel trumpet hear,—
  The news of heav'nly grace;
And, saved from earth, appear
  Before your Saviour's face :
The year of jubilee is come ;
Return, ye ransom'd sinners, home.

DELAY NOT, O SINNER. 11s.

1. De-lay not, de-lay not, O Sinner, draw near! The waters of life are now flowing for thee; No price is demanded, the Saviour is here, Redemption is purchas'd, salvation is free.
2. Delay not, delay not, O sinner, to come, For mercy still lingers, and calls thee to-day; Her voice is not heard in the vale of the tomb; Her message, unheeded, will soon pass away.
3. Delay not, delay not, the Spirit of Grace, Long griev'd and resisted, may take its sad flight, And leave thee in darkness to finish thy race, To sink in the vale of eternity's night.
4. Delay not, delay not, the hour is at hand, The earth shall dissolve, and the heavens shall fade; The dead, small and great, in the judgment shall stand; What pow'r then, O sinner shall lend thee its aid.

20. THE NEW YEAR.

1. Come, let us anew
 Our journey pursue,
 : Roll round with the year,:
 :And never stand still till the master appear!:

2 His adorable will
 Let us gladly fulfil,
 :And our talents improve,:   [love.:
 By the patience of hope and the labour of

3 Our life as a dream,
 Our time as a stream,
 :Glides swiftly away,:
 :And the fugitive moment refuses to stay ; :

4 O that each from his Lord
 May receive the glad word.
 ":Well and faithfully done!:[Throne.":
 : Enter into my joy, and sit down on my

EXPOSTULATION. 11s.

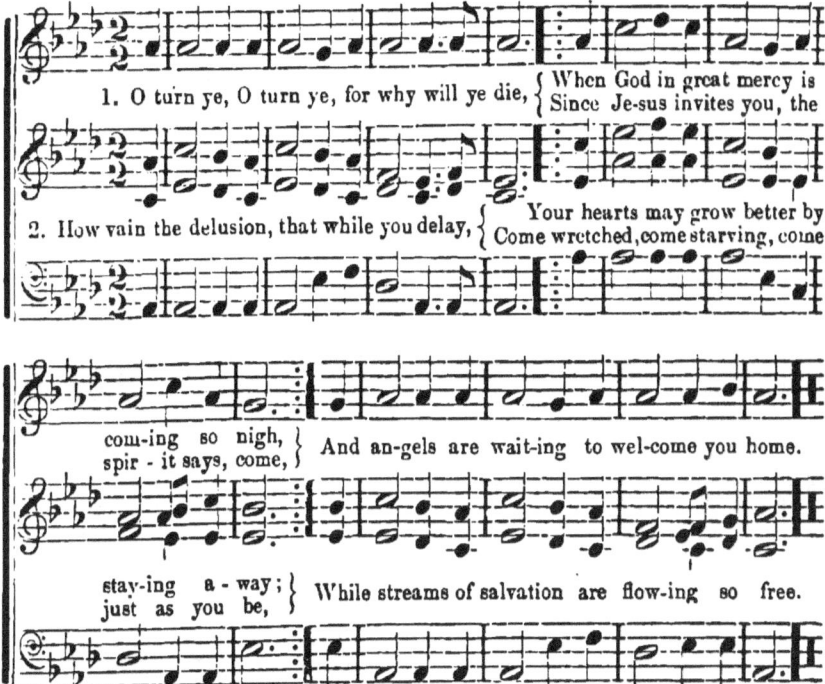

1. O turn ye, O turn ye, for why will ye die, { When God in great mercy is coming so nigh, Since Jesus invites you, the spirit says, come, } And angels are waiting to welcome you home.

2. How vain the delusion, that while you delay, { Your hearts may grow better by staying away; Come wretched, come starving, come just as you be, } While streams of salvation are flowing so free.

3
And now Christ is ready your souls to receive,
O how can you question, if you will believe?
If sin is your burden, why will you not come?
'Tis you he bids welcome; he bids you come home.

4
Come, give us your hand, and the Saviour your heart,
And trusting in heaven we never shall part:
O, how can we leave you? why will you not come?
We'll journey together, and soon be at home.

THE SABBATH.

How sweet is the Sabbath, the season of rest,
The day of the week which we surely love best!
This morning our Saviour arose from the tomb,
And took from the grave all its terror and gloom.

2
O, let us be thoughtful and prayerful to-day,
And not spend a moment in trifling or play!
Remembering the Sabbath was graciously given,
To draw us from earth, and prepare us for heaven.

REMEMBER THY CREATOR.

Acquaint yourselves early, dear children, with God,
And joy, like the sunshine, shall beam on your road;
And peace, like the dew-drops, shall fall on your head,
And sleep, like an angel, shall visit your bed.

2
Acquaint yourselves early, dear children, with God,
And he shall be with you when fears are abroad;
Your safeguard in dangers that threaten your path,
Your joy in the valley and shadow of death.

EVENING HYMN. 8s & 7s.

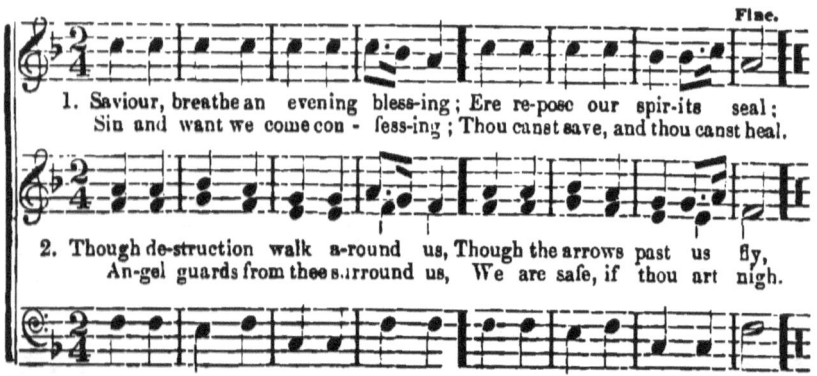

1. Saviour, breathe an evening bless-ing; Ere re-pose our spir-its seal;
Sin and want we come con - fess-ing; Thou canst save, and thou canst heal.

2. Though de-struction walk a-round us, Though the arrows past us fly,
An-gel guards from thee surround us, We are safe, if thou art nigh.

Sin and want we come con - fess ing,

Angel guards from thee surround us,

3
Though the night be dark and dreary,
  Darkness cannot hide from thee;
Thou art He who, never weary,
  Watchest where thy people be.

4
Should swift death this night o'ertake us,
  And command us to the tomb,
May the morn in heaven awake us,
  Clad in bright, eternal bloom.

BURIAL OF A CHRISTIAN BROTHER.

Brother, rest from sin and sorrow;
  Death is o'er, and life is won;
On thy slumber dawns no morrow:
  Rest; thine earthly race is run.

2
Brother, wake; the night is waning;
  Endless day is round thee poured;
Enter thou the rest remaining
  For the people of the Lord.

3
Brother, wake; for He who loved thee,—
He who died that thou mightst live,—
He who graciously approved thee,—
  Waits thy crown of joy to give.

4
Fare thee well; though woe is blending
  With the tones of earthly love,
Triumph high and joy unending
  Wait thee in the realms above.

THE FOUNT OF BLESSING.

Far from mortal cares retreating,
  Sordid hopes and vain desires,
Here, our willing footsteps meeting,
  Every heart to heaven aspires.

2
From the fount of glory beaming,
  Light celestial cheers our eyes,
Mercy from above proclaiming
  Peace and pardon from the skies.

3
Who may share this great salvation?
  Every poor and humble mind,
Every kindred, tongue, and nation,
  From the stains of guilt refined.

4
Blessings all around bestowing,
  God withholds his care from none,
Grace and mercy ever flowing
  From the fountain of his throne.

NO NIGHT IN HEAVEN.

5
No night shall be in Heaven—but endless noon;
No fast-declining sun, nor waning moon;
But there the Lamb shall yield perpetual light,
'Mid pastures green, and waters ever bright.

6
No night shall be in Heaven—no darkened room,
No bed of death, nor silence of the tomb;
But breezes, ever fresh with love and truth,
Shall brace the frame with an immortal youth,

7
No night shall be in Heaven! But night is here,
The night of sorrow, and the night of fear;
I mourn the ills that now my steps attend,
And shrink from others that may yet impend.

8
No night shall be in Heaven! O had I faith
To rest in what the faithful Witness saith,
That faith should make these hideous phantoms flee,
And leave no night, henceforth, on earth to me.

Tune on 102d page.

Swift my childhood's dreams are passing,
  Like the startled doves they fly,
Or bright clouds each other chasing
  Over yonder quiet sky.

2
Soon I'll hear earth's flattering story;
  Soon its visions will be mine,
Shall I covet wealth and glory?
  Shall I bow at pleasure's shrine?

3
No, my God: one prayer I raise thee
  From my young and happy heart;
Never let me cease to praise thee,
  Never from thy fear depart.

4
Then, when years have gathered o'er me,
  And the world is sunk in shade;
Heaven's bright realms will rise before me;
  There my treasure will be laid.

GOODWIN. 7s & 6s.

G. J. WEBB.

1. The morning light is breaking, The darkness disappears, The sons of earth are waking
D.C. Of nations in com-mo-tion,

2. Rich dews of grace come o'er us, In many a gentle shower, And brighter scenes before us
D.C. And heavenly gales are blowing,

To penitential tears. Each breeze that sweeps the ocean Brings tidings from a-far.
Prepared for Zion's war.

Are opening every hour: Each cry to heaven go-ing A-bund-ant answers brings,
With peace upon their wings.

PRAY WITHOUT CEASING.

Go when the morning shineth,
 Go when the noon is bright,
Go when the eve declineth,
 Go in the hush of night;
Go with pure mind and feeling,
 Fling earthly thought away,
And, in thy closet kneeling,
 Do, thou in secret pray.

2

Remember all who love thee,
 All who are loved by thee;
Pray, too, for those who hate thee,
 If any such there be;
Then for thyself, in meekness,
 A blessing humbly claim,
And blend with each petition
 Thy great Redeemer's name.

3

Or, if 'tis e'er denied thee
 In solitude to pray,
Should holy thoughts come o'er thee
 When friends are round thy way.

E'en then the silent breathing,
 Thy spirit raised above,
Will reach his throne of glory,
 Where dwells eternal love.

REMEMBER THY CREATOR.

"Remember thy Creator"
 While youth's fair spring is bright,
Before thy cares are greater,
 Before comes age's night;
While yet the sun shines o'er thee,
 While stars the darkness cheer,
While life is all before thee,
 Thy great Creator fear.

2

"Remember thy Creator"
 Ere life resigns its trust,
Ere sinks dissolving nature,
 And dust returns to dust;
Before with God, who gave it,
 The spirit shall appear;
He cries, who died to save it,
 "Thy great Creator fear."

THERE ARE ANGELS.

Arr. for this work.

1. There are an-gels hov'ring round, There are an-gels hov'ring round,
2. To carry the tidings home, To carry the tidings home,
3. To the new Je-ru-sa-lem, To the new Je-ru-sa-lem,
4. Poor sinners are coming home, Poor sinners are coming home,
5. And Je-sus bids them come, And Je-sus bids them come,

There are an - - gels, an - - gels hov-'ring round.
To car - - ry, car - - ry the ti - dings home.

To the new, the new Je - - ru - sa - lem.
Poor sin - - ners, sin - - ners are com - ing home.
And Je - - sus, Je - - sus bids them come.

JUST NOW.

Arr. for this Work.

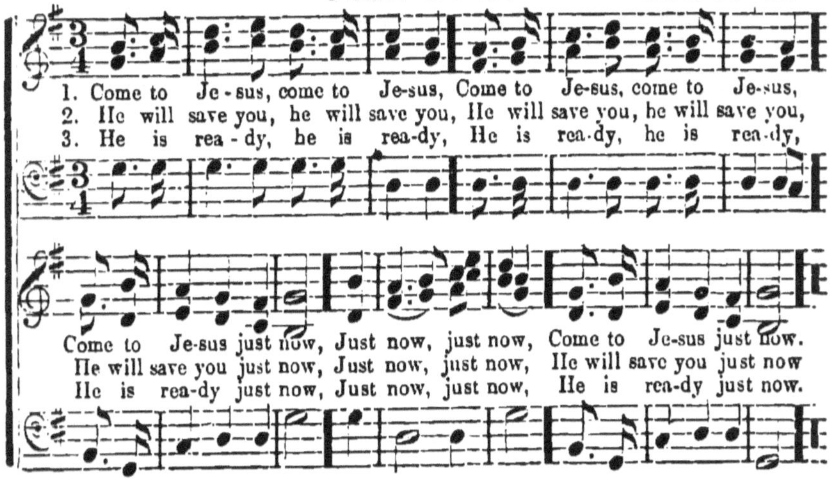

1. Come to Je-sus, come to Je-sus, Come to Je-sus, come to Je-sus,
2. He will save you, he will save you, He will save you, he will save you,
3. He is rea-dy, he is rea-dy, He is rea-dy, he is rea-dy,

Come to Je-sus just now, Just now, just now, Come to Je-sus just now.
He will save you just now, Just now, just now, He will save you just now.
He is rea-dy just now, Just now, just now, He is rea-dy just now.

BROWN. C. M.

W. B. BRADBURY.
From "The Jubilee." By permission.

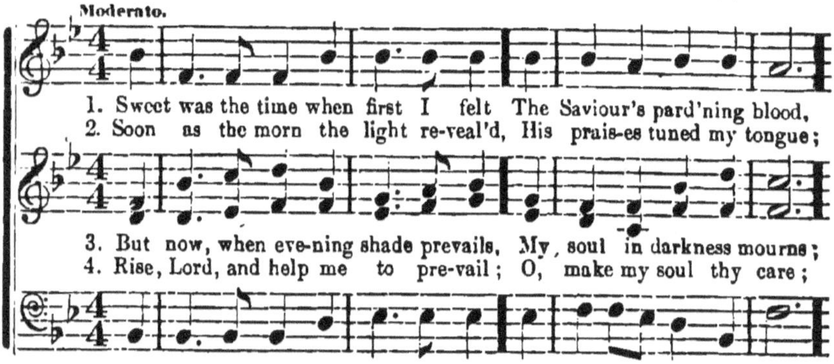

Moderato.

1. Sweet was the time when first I felt The Saviour's pard'ning blood,
2. Soon as the morn the light reveal'd, His praises tuned my tongue;
3. But now, when evening shade prevails, My soul in darkness mourns;
4. Rise, Lord, and help me to prevail; O, make my soul thy care;

Applied to cleanse my soul from guilt, And bring me home to God.
And when the evening shades prevail'd, His love was all my song.
And when the morning light reveals, No light to me returns.
I know thy mercies can-not fail; Let me that mercy share.

A PERFECT HEART THE REDEEMER'S THRONE.

O for a heart to praise my God,
  A heart from sin set free ;—
A heart that always feels thy blood,
  So freely spilt for me :—

2

A heart resign'd, submissive, meek,
  My great Redeemer's throne ;
Where only Christ is heard to speak,—
  Where Jesus reigns alone.

3

O for a lowly, contrite heart,
  Believing, true, and clean ;
Which neither life nor death can part
  From Him that dwells within :—

4

A heart in every thought renew'd,
  And full of love divine ;
Perfect, and right, and pure, and good,
  A copy, Lord, of thine.

LIGHT AND GLORY OF THE SACRED PAGE.

What glory gilds the sacred page!
  Majestic, like the sun,
It gives a light to every age ;
  It gives, but borrows none.

2

The power that gave it still supplies
  The gracious light and heat ;
Its truths upon the nations rise:
  They rise, but never set,

3

Lord ! everlasting thanks be thine
  For such a bright display,
As makes a world of darkness shine
  With beams of heavenly day.

4

Our souls rejoicingly pursue
  The steps of Him we love,
Till glory break upon our view
  In brighter worlds above.

ORTONVILLE. C. M.

DR. HASTINGS.
By permission.

107

1. Ma-jes-tic sweetness sits enthroned Up-on the Saviour's brow; His head with radiant glories crown'd, His lips with grace o'erflow, His lips, &c.
2. No mor-tal can with him com-pare A-mong the sons of men: Fairer is he than all the fair Who fill the heavenly train, Who fill the heavenly train.
3. He saw me plunged in deep dis-tress, And flew to my re-lief; For me he bore the shameful cross, And carried all my grief, And carried all my grief.
4. Since from his bounty I re-ceive Such proofs of love di-vine, Had I a thousand hearts to give, Lord they would all be thine, Lord they, &c.

THE RESOLUTION.

Come, humble sinner, in whose breast
  A thousand thoughts revolve,
Come, with your guilt and fear oppress'd,
  And make this last resolve:—

2

I'll go to Jesus, though my sin
  Like mountains round me close;
I know his courts, I'll enter in,
  Whatever may oppose.

3

Perhaps he will admit my plea,
  Perhaps will hear my prayer;
But, if I perish, I will pray,
  And perish only there.

4

I can but perish if I go—
  I am resolved to try;
For if I stay away, I know
  I must forever die.

THE SABBATH SCHOOL.

Sweet Sabbath school, place dear to me
  Where'er through life I roam,
My heart will often turn to thee,
  My childhood's Sabbath home.

2

Within thy courts of Him I've heard
  Whose birth the angels sung,
When o'er the shepherds, fill'd with fear,
  The star of glory hung.

3

O holy place! where first we shed
  The penitential tear;
Where youthful steps are taught to tread
  In paths of peace and prayer.

4

When all our wand'rings here shall cease,
  And cares of life shall end,
In God's eternal Sabbath place
  May we our anthems blend.

MEAR. C. M.

Arr. for this work.

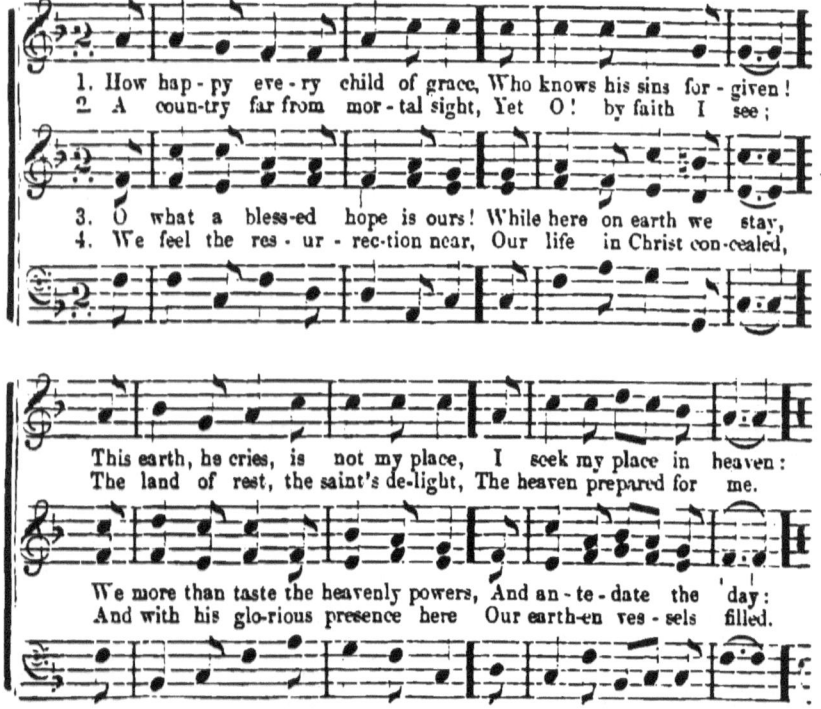

1. How happy every child of grace, Who knows his sins forgiven!
   This earth, he cries, is not my place, I seek my place in heaven:
2. A country far from mortal sight, Yet O! by faith I see;
   The land of rest, the saint's delight, The heaven prepared for me.
3. O what a blessed hope is ours! While here on earth we stay,
   We more than taste the heavenly powers, And antedate the day:
4. We feel the resurrection near, Our life in Christ concealed,
   And with his glorious presence here Our earthen vessels filled.

PRAYER FOR GUIDANCE.

O for a breeze of heavenly love,
  To waft our souls away,
To that celestial place above,
  Where pleasures ne'er decay,

2

Eternal Spirit, deign to be
  Our pilot here below,
To steer through life's tempestuous sea,
  When stormy winds do blow.

3

From rocks of pride on either hand,
  From quicksands of despair—
O guide us safe to Canaan's land,
  Through every latent snare.

4

Anchor us in that port above,
  On that celestial shore,
Where dashing billows never move,
  Where tempests never roar.

INFLUENCE EXERTED.

What if the little rain should say
  So small a drop as I
Can ne'er refresh the thirsty fields,
  I'll tarry in the sky?

2

What if a shining beam of noon
  Should in its fountain stay,
Because its feeble light alone
  Cannot create a day?

3

Doth not each rain-drop help to form
  The cool, refreshing shower?
And every ray of light, to warm
  And beautify the flower?

4

'Tis thus the good each child may do,
  When many do their best,
Will help to bring within our view
  The glory of the blest.

SILOAM. C. M.

I. B. WOODBURY.

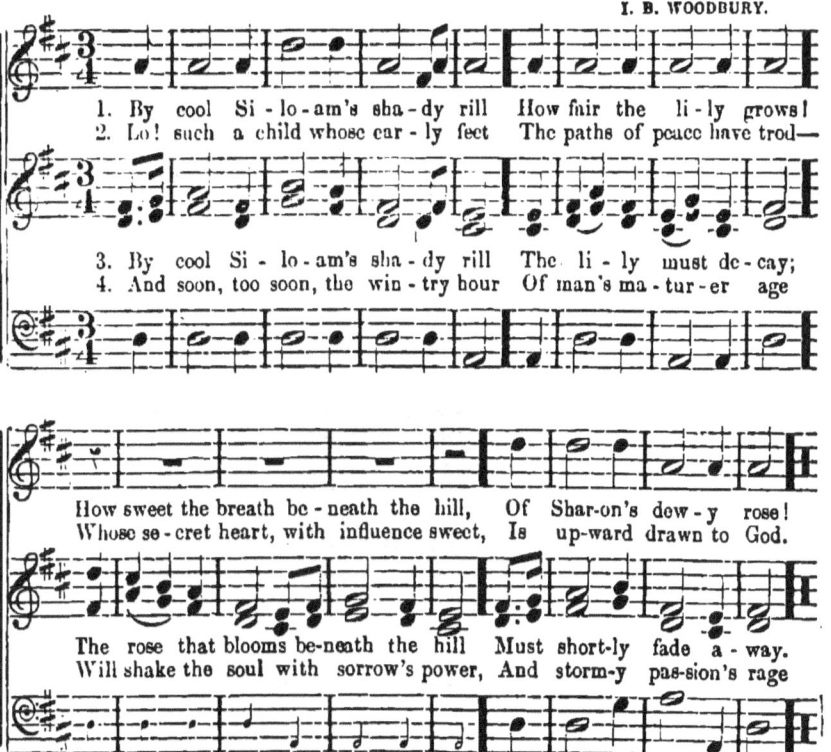

1. By cool Siloam's shady rill
How fair the lily grows!
How sweet the breath beneath the hill,
Of Sharon's dewy rose!

2. Lo! such a child whose early feet
The paths of peace have trod—
Whose secret heart, with influence sweet,
Is upward drawn to God.

3. By cool Siloam's shady rill
The lily must decay;
The rose that blooms beneath the hill
Must shortly fade away.

4. And soon, too soon, the wintry hour
Of man's maturer age
Will shake the soul with sorrow's power,
And stormy passion's rage.

PLEASURES OF TEACHING.

Be ours the bliss in wisdom's way,
  To guide untutored youth,
And lead the mind that went astray
  To virtue and to truth.

2

Delightful work, young souls to win,
  And turn the rising race
From the deceitful paths of sin,
  To seek redeeming grace!

3

Almighty God, thine influence shed
  To aid this good design;
The honors of thy name be spread,
  And all the glory thine.

STEADFAST FAITH.

My God, I know, I feel thee mine,
  And will not quit my claim,
Till all I have is lost in thine,
  And all renew'd I am.

2

I hold thee with a trembling hand,
  And will not let thee go,
Till steadfastly by faith I stand,
  And all thy goodness know.

A PRAYER FOR THE NATION.

O, guard our shores from every foe,
  With peace our border bless,
With prosperous times our cities crown,
  Our fields with plenteousness.

2

Unite us in the sacred love
  Of knowledge, truth, and thee;
And let our hills and valleys shout
  The songs of liberty.

3

Lord of the nations! thus to thee
  Our country we commend;
Thou art her refuge, thou her trust,
  Her everlasting friend.

ONWARD AND UPWARD.

REV. G. ROBBINS.
By permission.

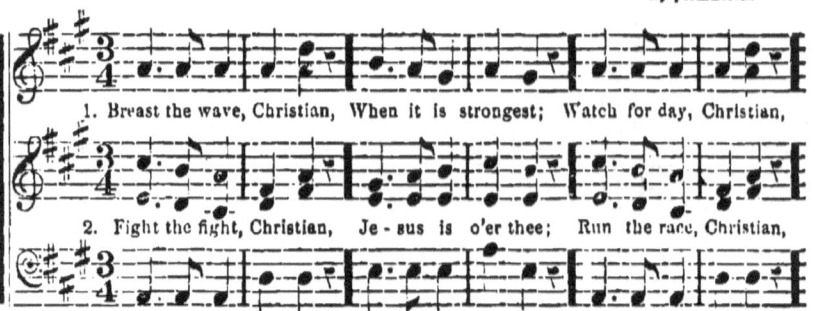

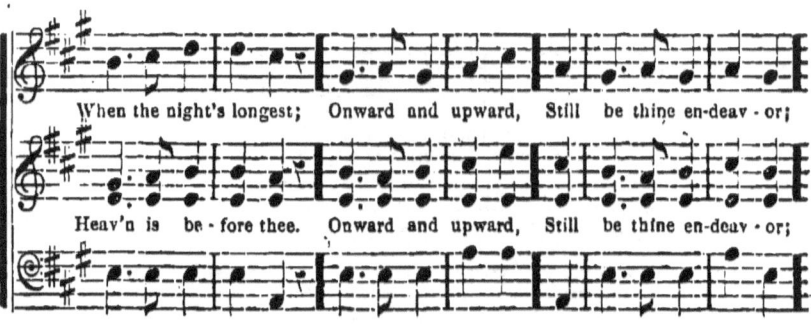

3
Bear the cross, Christian,
  Follow thy Master ;
Bright the crown, Christian,
  Haste thee on faster.
Onward and upward, &c.

4
Lift the eye, Christian,
  Just as it closeth ;
Raise the heart, Christian,
  Ere it reposeth ;
Onward and upward, &c.

PASSING AWAY.* C. M.

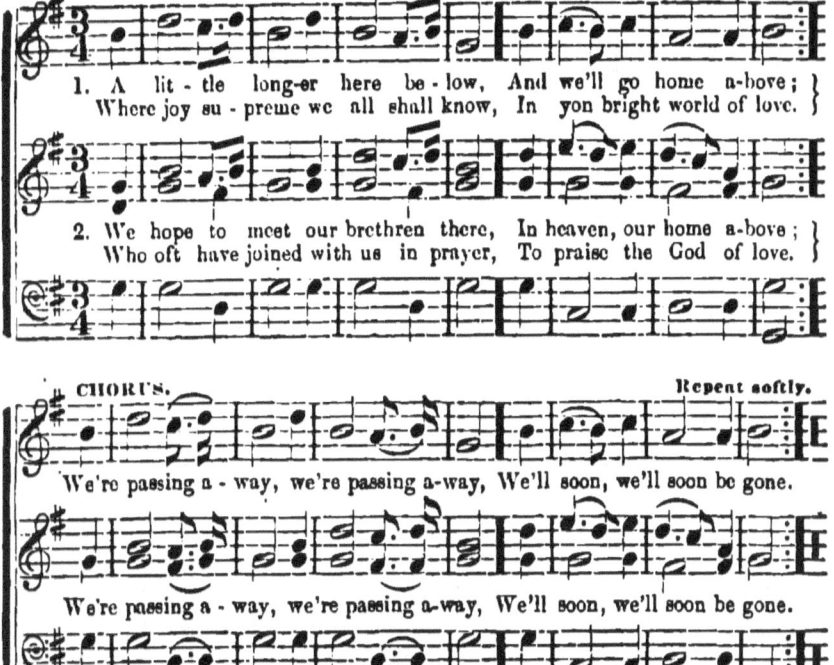

1. A lit-tle long-er here be-low, And we'll go home a-bove;
Where joy su-preme we all shall know, In yon bright world of love.

2. We hope to meet our brethren there, In heaven, our home above;
Who oft have joined with us in prayer, To praise the God of love.

CHORUS. *Repeat softly.*
We're passing a-way, we're passing a-way, We'll soon, we'll soon be gone.
We're passing a-way, we're passing a-way, We'll soon, we'll soon be gone.

3
Come, sinners come, to Christ and live,
There's peace for you above;
Forsake your sins and he'll forgive,
And all your guilt remove.
We're passing away, &c.

SHORTNESS OF TIME.
How fleeting are our moments here,
How soon the day is gone;
The morning sun soon reaches noon,
The night comes hastening on.
We're passing away, &c.

2
Oh life how vain, what trials prove,
And all that thou canst give,
But yonder is our home above,
Where we may always live.
We're passing away, &c.

3
What music sweet from heaven I hear,
Angelic forms I see,
Of parents, brothers, sisters dear,
They call, they call for me.
We're passing away, &c.

ANNIVERSARY HYMN.
Another year has passed away,
Time swiftly speeds along;
We come again to praise and pray,
And sing our greeting song.
CHO. We come again, we come again,
We come with song again.

2
We come the Saviour's name to praise,
To sing the wondrous love
Of Him who guards us all our days,
And guides to Heaven above.
We come, &c.

3
We'll sing of many a happy hour,
We've passed in Sunday school,
Where truth, like summer's genial showers,
Extends its gracious rule.
We come, &c.

4
Our youthful hearts will gladly raise,
Our voices sweetly sing
A general song of grateful praise,
To Heaven's eternal King.
We come, &c.

* Contributed by Dr. D. T. Huckins.

THE SUNDAY SCHOOL.

2.
Our Teachers true, we turn to you,
  As guides belov'd and kind ;
In youth and age, on mem'ry's page,
  Our thanks shall stand enshrined.
And when 'mid life's gay scenes we stray,
Where duties call, where passions play,
Your counsels wise, shall ever rise,
  Like guards around the mind.

3.
Our Pastor kind, we're e'er inclined
  To hear your gladsome voice ;
And fondly cling to truths you bring,
  They make our hearts rejoice.
And when these youthful days are past,
To riper joys and scenes we'll haste,
We'll gather where the good appear,
  And make their ways our choice.

* Or omit the Chorus and end here.

GREENWOOD. C. M. 113

Words by Rev. T. J. GREENWOOD.

114. THERE IS A PLACE OF SACRED REST. C. M.
Arranged.

3 Yes, even at that fearful hour,
   When death shall seize its prey,
   And from the place that knows us now,
   Shall hurry us away,—
The vision of that heavenly home
   Shall cheer the parting soul,
   And o'er it, mounting to the skies,
   A tide of rapture roll.

4 In that pure home of tearless joy
   Earth's parted friends shall meet,
   With smiles of love that never fade,
   And blessedness complete·
There, there adieus are sounds unknown
   Death frowns not on that scene,
   But life, and glorious beauty shine,
   Untroubled and serene.

PARTING. 6s & 5s. 115

1. When shall we meet again? Meet ne'er to sever? When will peace wreath her chain
2. When shall love freely flow Pure as life's river? When shall sweet friendship glow,
3. Up to that world of light Take us, dear Saviour; May we all there unite,
4. Soon shall we meet again—Meet ne'er to sever; Soon will peace wreath her chain,

Round us for-ev-er? Our hearts will ne'er re-pose Safe from each
Changeless for-ev-er? Where joys ce-les-tial thrill, Where bliss each
Hap-py for-ev-er: Where kindred spir-its dwell, There may our
Round us for-ev-er: Our hearts will then re-pose, Se-cure from

blast that blows In this dark vale of woes—Nev-er— no, nev-er!
heart shall fill, And fears of parting chill—Nev-er— no, nev-er!
mu-sic swell, And time our joys dis-pel, Nev-er— no, nev-er!
worldly woes; Our songs of praise shall close, Never— no, never!

THE SAVIOUR'S LOVE. C. M.

1. Dear Jesus, ever at my side, How loving must thou be;
To leave thy home in heaven to guard, A little child like me.
And, when my heart loves God, I know The sweetness is from thee.
I cannot feel thee touch my hand, With pressure light and mild.

2. But I have felt thee in my thoughts, Rebuking sin for me;
To check me as my mother did, When I was but a child.
Something there is within my heart, Which tells me thou art there.
And when, dear Saviour, I kneel down, Morning and night to prayer.

3 Yes! when I pray, thou prayest too—
  Thy prayer is all for me;
But when I sleep, thou sleepest not,
  But watchest patiently.
Dear Jesus, ever at my side,
  How loving must thou be,
To leave thy home in heaven, to guard
  A little child like me.

THE PROSPECT JOYOUS.

1 O what hath Jesus bought for me!
  Before my ravish'd eyes
Rivers of life divine I see,
  And trees of paradise :
I see a world of spirits bright,
  Who taste the pleasures there ;
They all are robed in spotless white,
  And conqu'ring palms they bear.

2 O what are all my suff'ring's here,
  If, Lord, thou count me meet
With that enraptured host t' appear,
  And worship at thy feet !
Give joy or grief, give ease or pain,
  Take life or friends away,
But let me find them all again
  In that eternal day.

GOING HOME. 117

1. Whither, pil-grims are you go-ing, Each one on his way?
2. Fear ye not the way so lone-ly, You a fee-ble band?
3. Tell me pil-grims what you hope for, In that bet-ter Land?
4. Will you let me jour-ney with you, To that bet-ter land?

We are on our heavenly jour-ney, All of us to day.
No, for friends un-seen are near us, An-gels round us stand.

Spot-less robes and crowns of glo-ry, From our Saviour's hand.
Come a-long, we bid you wel-come, To our hap-py band.

CHORUS to each verse.

Go-ing, go-ing, to our heavenly home.
Sing-ing, sing-ing, sing-ing as we go.

THE HEAVENLY JOURNEY.

We are going, going, going,
　To a land of light ;
Where are flowing, flowing, flowing,
　Waters pure and bright. Going, &c.

2

We are singing, singing, singing,
　As we pass along ;

Hear the ringing, ringing, ringing,
　Of triumphant song. Going, &c.

3

Jesus, Saviour, leave us never,
　May we faithful prove ;
Then at home with thee forever.
　Gathered be above. Going, &c.

SWEET HEAVEN.

(COMMON METRE.) *Arranged by A. HULL.*

1. O hap-py land! O hap-py land! Where saints and an-gels dwell;
3. Thou heavenly Friend! thou heavenly Friend! O hear us when we pray;

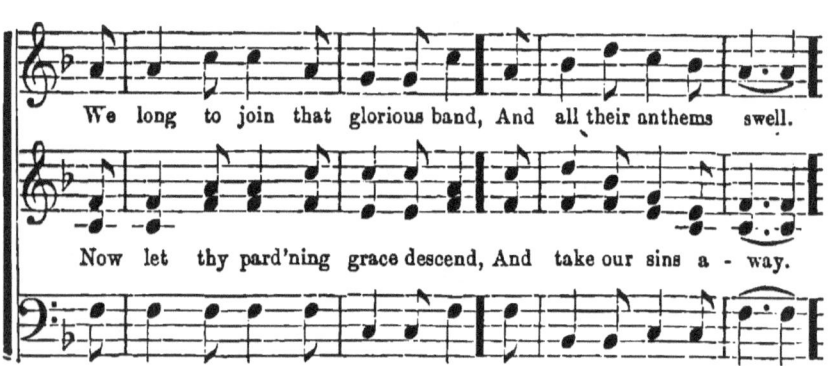

We long to join that glorious band, And all their anthems swell.
Now let thy pard'ning grace descend, And take our sins a-way.

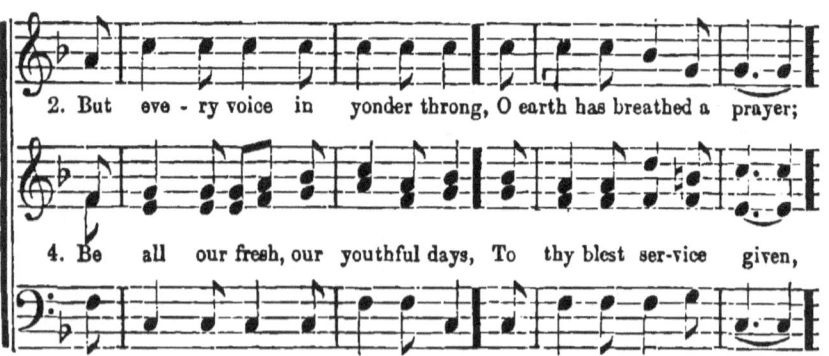

2. But eve-ry voice in yonder throng, O earth has breathed a prayer;
4. Be all our fresh, our youthful days, To thy blest ser-vice given,

CHILDHOOD'S PRAYER.

Words by Rev. T. J. GREENWOOD. Music arranged by LESLIE.

GATHER THEM INTO OUR SUNDAY SCHOOL. 123

Words and Music arr. by J. P. SAMUEL.

DUET.
Gather them in from the broad highway; Gather them in in this Gospel day;
Gather them in from the prairies vast; Gather them in of ev - e - ry cast.

TRIO.
Ga-ther them in—let my house be full; Gather them in-to our Sunday School.

CHORUS.
Gather them in— gather them in; Gather them in to our Sunday School.

2 Gather them in in numbers . . ;
  Gather them in, both young and old;
  Gather them in from the widow's home;
  Gather them in that sigh and groan.
    Cho. Gather them in, &c.

3 Gather them in from the street and lane;
  Gather them in, both halt and lame;
  Gather the deaf, the poor, the blind,—
  Gather them in with a willing mind.
    Cho. Gather them in, &c.

4 Gather them in that seek for rest,—
  Gather them in from East to West;
  Gather them in that wander about,—
  Gather them in from North to South.
    Cho. Gather them in, &c.

5 Gather them in from all the land,
  Gather them into our noble band;
  Gather them in with Christian love,—
  Gather them in for the Church above.
    Cho. Gather them in, &c.

INDEX OF FIRST LINES.

A charge to keep I have..35, 84
According to thy gracious.. 59
Afflictions though they.... 54
A home in heaven, what a.. 27
Alas, and did my Saviour.. 60
All hail the power of Jesus' 86
A little longer here below..111
Am I a soldier of the....41, 68
And can I yet delay....... 84
Another six days' work is.. 22
As oft we here get weary.. 24
Arise, my soul, arise...... 98
Awake, my soul, in joyful.. 39

Blow ye the trumpet, blow. 99
Brother, rest from sin and..102
Breast the wave............110

Cease ye mourners, cease.. 79
Children of the heavenly.. 34
Come let us anew our......100
Come thou fount of.....31, 79
Come sinners to the gospel. 92
Come ye that love the...35, 63
Come, Holy Spirit, heaven. 44
Come let us join our 56
Come, poor pilgrim, sad and 15
Come to the house of prayer 85
Come let us lift our joyful.. 59
Come ye sinners, poor and. 74
Come to Jesus just now...105
Come, humble sinner, in...107
Come, poor sinner, come to 77
Come, weary sinners...... 53
Crown his head with....... 75

Delay not, delay not, O....100
Depth of mercy, can there. 71

Far from these scenes of..53, 83
Far from mortal cares.....102
Father, whate'er of carthly 63
From all that dwell below... 19
From Greenland's icy..... 67
From whence doth this.... 97
Forever with the Lord..... 80

Gently Lord, O gently lead 78
Give me the wings of faith. 62
God is the refuge of his... 26
God is love: his mercy.... 75
God of mercy, hear our.... 73
God moves in a mysterious 63
Go when the morning......104
Great God, to thee my..... 77
Great Jehovah, we adore... 77
Guide me, O thou great.... 76
Great God, attend while... 23

Hark! the bell to prayer is 6
Hark, the voice of love and 77
Haste, O sinner, now be... 34
How fleeting are our.......111
How happy every child of..108

How vain is all beneath... 25
How pleasant, how divinely 22
How sweet the name of.... 28
How sweet the hour of.... 94
How blest the righteous.... 90
How sweet, how heavenly. 62
How sweet is the Sabbath..101
Holy Father, we adore thee 76

If we knew while here as.. 12
If human kindness meets... 61
If through unruffled seas... 10
I have a home beyond the.. 39
I long to behold him....... 9
I love the Lord; he heard.. 63
I love to steal awhile away. 69
I'll praise my maker with.. 46
I'm not ashamed to own my 56
In the Christian's home in. 30
I'm but a stranger here.... 51
I would not live alway, I... 45
I was a wand'ring sheep... 11
I want a heart to pray..... 81

Jesus and shall it ever be.. 25
Jesus died on Calvary's.... 36
Jesus, lover of my soul.... 25
Jesus shall reign where'er.. 19
Jesus, I my cross have taken 64
Jesus my all to heaven is.. 4
Joyfully, joyfully, onward I 47
Just as I am, without one.. 18
Just as thou art—without.. 18

Know, my soul, thy full.... 64

Like Israel, Lord, am I..... 82
Lo! the gospel ship is...... 65
Lord, in the morning thou. 87
Lord of hosts, how lovely.. 73
Lord, we come before thee. 73
Lord! I delight in thee..... 81
Lord, dismiss us with thy.. 74
Love divine, all love excel. 17

Majestic sweetness sits....107
Meet again! when life is... 48
Must Jesus bear the cross.. 56
My heavenly home is bright 92
My heart is fixed on thee.. 26
My Saviour, fill my soul... 82
My soul repeat his praise.. 85
My God, I know I feel thee 109

No night shall be in heaven 103

Of him who did salvation.. 22
O for a heart to praise..89, 106
O for a thousand tongues.. 43
O for a shout of joy....... 83
Oh! I have roamed through 33
O happy day that fixed my 5
O for a breeze of heavenly.108
O happy land, O happy....115
O Jesus, delight of my soul 97

O Jesus, my Saviour, to.... 43
O land of rest, for thee I... 21
On Jordan's stormy.....57, 89
O turn ye, O turn ye, for..101
O 'tis delight without alloy. 68
Out on an ocean all bound. 38
O when shall I see Jesus... 49
O where shall rest be...... 53
O what has Jesus bought..116
O guard our (National)....109
Praise God, from whom all. 93
Praise to God, immortal... 72
Praise the Lord; ye heavens 75
People of the living God... 84

Roll on, thou mighty ocean 67

Saviour, breathe an....79, 102
Serene I laid me down..... 82
Shall we meet beyond the.. 7
Should sorrow o'er thy.... 52
Sinner turn, why will you.. 29
Sinner go, will you go..... 42
Sinner, the voice of God... 21
Silently the shades of...... 17
Softly fades the twilight ray 72
Spare us, O Lord, aloud we 91
Sweet 'tis to sing of thee... 8
Sweet the moments, rich in 16
Sweet was the time when..106
Sweet is the work, O Lord! 40
Sweet is the work, my..... 23

That awful day will surely. 59
The angels now are calling. 50
The day has come, the..... 55
The mellow eve is gliding.. 66
The morning light is.......104
The Lord my pasture shall. 95
The hill of Zion yields..... 35
The pity of the Lord....... 84
There are ange's hov'ring..105
There is a land of pure.... 89
There is a fountain filled... 41
There is a happy land..... 14
There is an hour of peaceful 69
There is a place of sacred..114
There's not a star whose... 32
Thou that dost my life..... 72
Thou dear Redeemer, dying 58
To Jesus, the crown of my. 96
Tossed upon life's raging... 65
The world is overcome by.. 8

Vain man, thy fond........ 60

Welcome, sweet day of.... 85
We live as pilgrims and.... 00
We speak of the realms of. 97
We'll not give up the Bible. 88
We're bound for the land.. 37
We're going, going, going..117
When I can read my title.. 32
When shall the voice of.... 67
When I survey the wond.. 94

INDEX OF FIRST LINES.

When the worn spirit wants 61
When shall we meet again. 115
What glory gilds the........ 106
What sinners value I resign 93
What various hindrances... 90
What now is my object.... 97
While life prolongs its..... 90
Whither, pilgrims, are you. 117
Who are these in bright.... 70
Why should our tears in... 61
Why should we boast of... 60
Within thy house, O Lord.. 87
With stately towers and... 87

Yet there is room for thy.. 20
Yes, we'll meet beyond the 13

SABBATH SCHOOL HYMNS.

Acquaint yourselves early.. 101
Another year has passed... 111
Be ours the bliss in......... 109
By cool Siloam's shady rill. 109
Children, hear the melt.. 74, 77
Dear Jesus, ever at my.... 116
Father, who art in heaven. 120
Gather them in from the... 123
I love the Sabbath School.. 32
If we knew while walking. 13
In life's bright morning the 38
I want to be an angel..... 48
I would a youthful pilgrim. 5
Joyful, joyful, joyful be.... 126
Kind words can never die.. 9
Little travellers Zionward.. 29

Little schoolmates, can you 48
O happy land, O happy... 118
Remember thy Creator..... 104
See the leaves around us... 66
Sweet Sabbath School..... 107
Swift my childhood dreams 108
The Sunday School with.. 112
The Bible, the Bible, more. 45
The Sabbath sheds its..... 113
This morning, Lord, attend 40
We'll not give up the Bible. 58
What if the little rain..... 106
Whither, pilgrim, are you.. 117
When in the Sabbath...... 62

TEMPERANCE HYMNS.

Onward speed thy conquer. 124
Oh! bright is the wine.... 125

INDEX OF TUNES.

A Home in Heaven..P. M. 27
Arise, my soul, arise.H. M. 98

Balerma ....C. M. 63
Brown..............C. M. 106
Boylston............S. M. 84

Come, thou fount..8 & 7s. 31
Consolation........L. M. 26
Complaint..........L. M. 91
Come to Jesus......C. M. 20
Claremont.........8 & 7s. 16
Cross and Crown....C. M. 56
Coming home.......C. M. 55
Childhood's prayer........ 120
Coronation.........C. M. 86

Dear Saviour.......L. M. 4
Defence..............7s. 28
Delay not..........11s. 100
Depth of mercy......7s. 71
Dundee.............C. M. 60
Disciple...........8 & 7s. 64

Eden is my home....C. M. 33
Evening Hymn.....8 & 7s. 102
Emmons.............C. M. 68
Exhortation........C. M 57
Expostulation......11s. 101
Evening Shades....8 & 7s. 17

Florence............L. M. 25
Freeport............L. M. 19
Forever with the Lord. S. M. 80

Going Home............... 117
God is love........8 & 7s. 75
Goodwin...........7 & 6s. 104
Greenville........8 & 7s. 77
Gently, Lord.....8 & 7s. 78
Glory to the Lamb......... 3
Gather them into......... 123
Greenwood................ 113
Heaven is my home........ 51

Homeward bound.......... 38
Holy Father.....8, 7 & 4s. 76

I'm going home.....L. M. 39
I do believe.........C. M. 41
I would not live alway.11s. 45
I long to behold him...8s. 9
If we knew.............. 12

Joyfully................. 47
Just now................ 105
Just as I am......L. M. 18
Joyful be our numbers.... 126
Jesus our friend.......... 8

Lebanon............L. M. 23
Long time ago.....6 & 4s. 36

Mount Auburn......L. M. 22
Madison.............8s. 96
Morning Hymn...S. M. 82
Marlow.............C. M. 59
Meet Again...........7s. 48
Mear................C. M. 106
My heavenly home..L. M. 93

Newton.............L. M. 92
Northfield.........C. M. 43
No night in heaven........ 103

Old Hundred.......L. M. 93
O land of rest......C. M. 21
O 'tis delight.......C. M. 68
O when shall I....7 & 6s. 49
Onward and Upward....... 110
Onward speed....(Temp.) 124
Ortonville ....C. M. 107

Passing Away............. 111
Parting................. 115
Praise 7s. 72
Pleyel's Hymn........7s. 73
Peterboro'.........C. M. 62
Phillips...........C. M. 61

Rest in Heaven........6s. 52
Rest for the weary.8 & 7s. 30

Ship of Canaan....8 & 7s. 65
Shall we meet....8 & 7s. 7
Salvation's free....S. M. 83
Siloam.............C. M. 109
Submission........S. M. 10
St. Thomas........S. M. 85
Shun the cup.....(Temp.) 125
Sicily............8, 7 & 4s. 74
Sweet Heaven......C. M. 118
Sweet rest in heaven...... 24
Sweet is the work...S. M. 40

The angels are calling.... 50
The Invitation............ 6
The Wanderer.......S. M. 11
The Eden above........... 37
The mellow eve....7 & 6s. 66
The Prodigal.......C. M. 54
The Good Shepherd.L. M. 95
The happy land........... 14
The hill of Zion....S. M. 35
The pilgrim's song......7s. 84
The sinner's invitation.... 42
The Saviour's Love..C. M. 116
The Sunday School....... 112
There's not a star....C. M. 32
There is a place....C M. 114
Turner.............C. M. 44
There are angels.......... 105
There, there is rest....... 15

Universal Praise..L. P. M. 46

Warwick...........C. M. 87
We'll not give up....C. M. 88
Ward..............L. M. 90
Who are these in....7s. 70
Woodland..........C. M. 69

Yes, we'll meet....8 & 7s. 13
Zephyr.............L. M. 94

www.ingramcontent.com/pod-product-compliance
Lightning Source LLC
Chambersburg PA
CBHW020113170426
43199CB00009B/519